# Property: A window of opportunity

By Stephen Church

## Legal Disclaimer

The information in this book is offered as a guide only. The examples and figures reflect non-specific market conditions. I have made them as accurate and as relevant as possible at the time of writing. However, the content, projections, figures and indications contained in this book are based on my experience and judgment alone. I cannot accept liability for decisions made based on the contents of this book, nor should not be relied upon when making investment decisions. I would advise anyone planning on making a property investment to seek legal and financial advice from qualified advisors before making any commitments. All rights reserved. No part of this publication may be reproduced, distributed, or transmitted in any form or by any means, including photocopying, recording, or other electronic or mechanical methods without the prior written permission of the publisher except for brief quotations embodied in critical reviews.

Copyright © 2017 by Stephen Church

Acknowledgements

First and foremost, I would like to thank my parents, John and June, for their continued guidance in life. I would also like to thank my sisters, Susane and Christina, for proving beyond a doubt that life's hardships can be overcome. You are an inspiration to many. I would also like to thank my brother, Ben, for showing me that you can have more than one passion in life. So, perhaps one day I will take up fishing!

Above all, I want to thank my wife, Lauryane, and our son, Raphaël. Thanks for being part of my journey. We don't have a destination, only an end.

Last, but not least, I would like to thank all those friends who have provided support and encouragement over the years. The rest know who you are. Happy investing.

This book is dedicated to the memory of my grandparents. Perhaps it was their enduring wisdom or the sign above the mantelpiece, which read: 'I CAN, I WILL' that provided the foundation of belief in myself.

## Preface

This book came about for one simple reason—I have a passion for property. Moreover, I have always taken great pleasure in providing impartial advice to anyone who asks. As the advice being given in this regard began to escalate, it seemed a natural progression to put pen to paper and share my experiences in investing in property. Having been fortunate enough to travel at a young age and own properties in several countries, I am able to explain the highs and lows of property investment as it applies to generating passive income. So, what can you expect? Well, there are no nail-biting twists or turns, no cunning book plot, heroes or villains—depending on your view of banks. Instead, this book is primarily aimed at the novice property investor (which isn't to say that some seasoned investors couldn't still learn a thing or two). Property investing is about planning for the future and ultimately creating a financial nest egg for you and your family, wherever in the world you live, or plan to live. When it comes to property investing for the future, I will guide you through the pitfalls and mistakes made by many, including myself, so that you don't have make the same costly errors.

I am confident that by the end of the book you will have a good understanding of how property investing can be done.

I'll do my best to direct you and provide you with the necessary information to build passive income and, ultimately, financial independence. Along the way, I will also recount some of my personal experiences and provide some working examples. After all, life is a journey, not a destination, and we never stop learning.

As historian Daniel Boorstin once said, 'Education is learning what you didn't even know you didn't know'.

## Table of Contents

| | | |
|---|---|---|
| 1 | The Question | 1 |
| 2 | Passive Income | 1 |
| 3 | Having a Passion | 2 |
| 4 | Financial Freedom | 4 |
| 5 | Living Longer | 4 |
| 6 | Property is a Business | 6 |
| 7 | Self-employment | 7 |
| 8 | Why Property? | 8 |
| 9 | Long-term Rentals | 10 |
| 10 | The 9–5 Job | 10 |
| 11 | Time | 13 |
| 12 | Getting a Foot on the Ladder | 14 |
| 13 | Getting Started: Considerations | 15 |
| 14 | Start Sooner Rather than Later | 17 |
| 15 | How Many Properties Should I Buy? | 17 |
| 16 | Capital Appreciation | 19 |
| 17 | Investment Strategy | 20 |
| | • Residential | 21 |
| | • Commercial | 21 |
| | • Industrial | 22 |
| 18 | Which Type of Property to Start With? | 23 |
| 19 | The First Step | 24 |
| 20 | Net Worth | 25 |

| 21 | The Search | 31 |
| --- | --- | --- |
| 22 | Value Added Property | 33 |
| 23 | The Deposit | 33 |
| 24 | Loan-to-value (LTV) | 34 |
| 25 | Speculating | 37 |
| 26 | Buying Expensive Properties | 37 |
| 27 | Student Housing | 39 |
| 28 | Debt-to-income Ratio | 40 |
| 29 | Online Information | 41 |
| 30 | Freehold versus Leasehold | 43 |
| 31 | Exhibitions: Another Source of Information | 44 |
| 32 | Stocks and Shares versus Property | 46 |
| 33 | Property Values: A Brief History | 51 |
| 34 | The Property Cycle | 53 |
| 35 | Appreciation Creates Equity | 57 |
|  | • Scenario 1: Cross-collateralised | 63 |
|  | • Scenario 2: Alternative Lender | 65 |
| 36 | Buying versus Long-term Renting | 66 |
| 37 | Good Debt versus Bad Debt | 70 |
| 38 | Borrowing | 73 |
| 39 | Banks | 77 |
| 40 | More on Mortgage Brokers | 78 |
| 41 | Mortgages | 81 |
| 42 | Islamic Mortgages | 88 |
| 43 | Principal and Interest | 90 |
| 44 | Loan Pre-approval | 91 |
| 45 | Refinancing | 91 |

| 46 | Mortgage Payments | 94 |
| 47 | Create Your Own Mortgage Calculator | 96 |
| 48 | The 1% Rule | 98 |
| 49 | Location | 98 |
| 50 | Don't Sell | 100 |
| 51 | Leveraging or Gearing | 106 |
| 52 | Gross Potential Income | 108 |
| 53 | Gross Rental Yields | 112 |
| 54 | Net Rental Yields | 113 |
| 55 | Vacancy/Voids | 117 |
| 56 | Net Operating Income | 121 |
| 57 | Capitalisation Rate | 122 |
| 58 | The Tenants | 128 |
| 59 | Keeping Track of the Rentals | 129 |
| 60 | Tenancy Contracts | 130 |
| 61 | Viewings | 131 |
| 62 | Breakeven | 134 |
| 63 | Gross Rent Multiplier (GRM) | 137 |
| 64 | Buying Overseas | 138 |
| 65 | Holiday Lets | 140 |
| 66 | Net Operating Income (NOI) | 148 |
| 67 | Cash Flow (before Tax) | 149 |
| 68 | Cash-on-Cash | 149 |
| 69 | Gross and Net Yields | 155 |
| 70 | Net Present Value | 163 |
| 71 | Making an Offer | 170 |
| 72 | What Happens after Finding a Property? | 172 |

| | | |
|---|---|---|
| 73 | Existing and Tenanted Investment Property | 175 |
| 74 | The Purchase | 182 |
| 75 | Motivated Sellers | 184 |
| 76 | Ripple Effect | 186 |
| 77 | Setting your Goals | 186 |
| 78 | Losing Focus | 187 |
| 79 | Setting Up as a Company | 189 |
| 80 | Insurance | 191 |
| 81 | Finding the Right Properties | 194 |
| 82 | Buying and Renovating | 195 |
| 83 | Property Secrets | 200 |
| 84 | The Property Business Question | 202 |
| 85 | Frank and Betty: The Investors | 202 |
| 86 | Building the Passive Income | 212 |
| 87 | Start by Renting, not Buying | 218 |
| 88 | Invest Further or Pay Down Loans? | 221 |
| 89 | Some Golden Rules | 225 |

## 1   The Question

Imagine a room filled with 100 people. Their ages range from 20 to 60. I ask them one simple question: 'Please raise your hand if your answer is yes to the following question: if you could set a goal that would enable you to retire early while providing enough income to sustain your desired lifestyle, would you?' How many hands would go up? More importantly, would you have raised yours? While the room could be almost anywhere in the world, I am confident that the response would invariably be the same—a resounding yes. However, to achieve this goal, we need a source of income or, preferably, a source of passive income.

## 2   Passive Income

*Investopedia* defines passive income as 'earnings an individual derives from a rental property, limited partnership or another enterprise in which he or she is not actively involved'. Popular culture, however, defines it as 'any money you earn while sitting on a beach sipping mojitos'. I like the latter, but it's unfortunately not that easy.

A more accurate definition would perhaps be that 'passive income is the money you earn from a project or investment after you've made an initial contribution of time or money'. We shall look at passive income from this perspective.

When you start acquiring properties, otherwise known as real estate for investment purposes, your ultimate goal is to earn a profit through both cash flow and appreciation.

## 3   Having a Passion

Some people have a passion for cars or fishing, others for music or sports. I just happen to have a passion for property. The dynamics of property are constantly evolving. It's an exciting industry. I am also fortunate in that my wife shares my passion (admittedly not as strongly). As a bonus, she also has a gift for interior design. You don't have to be passionate about property to invest and create passive income, but I believe it helps. With the exception of perhaps a few individuals, I am confident in predicting that you have, on several occasions, wished that you had enough money to do what you want, when you want. In other words, you've wished for financial freedom. It's one of the reasons we work. It's the same reason that would have caused you to raise your hand. There is nothing wrong with an honest day's work and the gratification it gives us. But, for most of us, that gratification comes in the form of a salary. So, the question is whether the salary (active income) is able to provide the financial freedom and allow you to achieve the lifestyle goals you really desire. In this book, I will reveal the must-knows to building a profitable property portfolio that will help you to achieve both your financial and lifestyle goals. This book will guide you through the steps to accomplishing those goals. You should find it surprisingly straightforward. The best part is that you don't need to have any specialised knowledge or skills. Furthermore, your passive income will grow over time. Depending on how you build your property portfolio, you should reach a point where you can stop working (assuming you want to), because the passive income generated will eventually exceed your active income. This means you will finally have the time and the money to live life the way you want.

What you should learn by reading this book is how to select and evaluate the right investment properties. Why? Because you have only two resources—money and time—and the only one that is truly limited is time. We can influence and change many variables in life, but we cannot turn back the clock. As potential investors, this means that the sooner you start the better, preferably by your mid-twenties. While this is the optimum age to begin investing, it does not mean that it's too late if you are in your forties or fifties. Our goal is to build a stream of passive income and achieve financial freedom earlier rather than later in life.

## 4 Financial Freedom

So what does financial freedom provide?

- The option to retire early (at least from your day job).
- The freedom to travel. It's a wonderful world out there, so go and explore!
- More family time. Or rather, more quality family time.
- The financial means and freedom to work for charitable causes.
- Greater buying power. Money doesn't buy happiness, but it can be used to support your needs, big or small.
- A less stressful life.

Of course, having financial freedom means different things to different people. So, what constitutes financial freedom, or, as some would say, wealth? Only one person can really answer that question—you!

## 5 Living Longer

One consideration for securing your financial future is your life expectancy. The good news is that we are living longer. The world average is around 67 years, with, for example, the UAE at 77 and France at 82. Life expectancy at birth now exceeds 84 years in Japan—the current leader—and is at least 81 years in several other countries, including the UK.

This means those in their early twenties can hopefully look forward to living longer lives. However, with only a state pension for many, longevity might not be as rewarding as it could be. Many young people look only at the present, not to the future, and they certainly don't ponder their retirement years. I am sure that many see themselves succeeding in life and becoming wealthy, or at least comfortable. I don't blame them, for I was the same. But is that realistic? Wealth is a relative term, so there is no definitive answer to that question. However, having travelled that road for several years, it's apparent that the illusions of many will be shattered. I don't know anyone who wouldn't want to live longer. Therefore, all I am suggesting is that a little planning and investment now can make positive life changes for the future. I'll show you how.

To put it bluntly, property investment potential comes down to the numbers. In this case, the numbers are the cash flow. The cash flow is simply income and expenses. If you don't analyse these investment numbers prior to making a purchase, then you could end up with a negatively geared investment, which means losing money. The internet is full of 'get-rich-quick' schemes, offering near-instant wealth—at least that's what they would like you to believe. But I can assure you that it's not that simple. Nothing in life comes easily. Property investing does take time and effort. This book will show you how to optimise those efforts. Don't waste your time or money on schemes that are too good to be true.

## 6 Property is a Business

Property investing is a business just like any other. To be successful, you must understand the fundamentals. What do you think would happen if I gifted USD 60,000 in cash to 10 random strangers and asked them to buy the best investment property they could find for the money? It's an interesting question.

I know one thing for certain: the outcome would be diverse, as each would take a slightly, or perhaps radically, different approach.

Most would seek properties in and around the area in which they live. That's fine, but let's not forget that some areas outperform others.

A few would look online for the best deal they could find. Most would seek a property as close to the USD 60,000 limit as possible.

Some would perhaps go to an estate agent and ask for the best deal possible for the USD 60,000 they have to invest.

One or two might even go to an auction hoping to bag a bargain.

What would you do? I will pose the same question again later in the book. Hopefully, you will learn a thing or two along the way that will influence your response. Think about what you might do now, and compare that to the answer you will give later.

## 7 Self-employment

I think it is fair to say that, with the exception of a few, most people would like to be self-employed. In other words, work for yourself. It means you make the plans, and you set your daily timetable. It means you answer to no one but yourself. It means you take control of your life. It gives you freedom. But most people work for a company, so their choices are limited. Generating income from passive investment, however, can provide you with choice. The greater the income the greater the choice, and, ultimately, the greater the financial freedom. There is no magic number of properties that you need to own. If you decide to follow my advice and build up your rental property portfolio, the numbers will speak for themselves. One day, you will realise that you earn more from managing your rental properties than from your 9–5 job. Of course, nothing prevents you from doing both.

## 8   Why Property?

Let's start with the obvious question: 'Why property?' If you are looking to become wealthy or just have a modest income, these goals can be achieved in any number of ways. Starting your own business would seem an obvious one. But that's reliant on finding a niche market to fulfil customer needs and build a profitable company. It can take years of very hard work. Moreover, global statistics clearly indicate that most businesses will fail within their first three years, so the financial risks of starting your own business are very high and often very costly.

Investing in a property to create a stream of passive income, on the other hand, is a great way to build a solid portfolio over the medium to long term, and that's the key. As I said, this is not a get-rich-quick scheme; it takes time. Passive income is the money you earn from a project or investment after you've made an initial contribution of time or money. This could be earnings from past investments or perhaps ones you are still making. Active income, on the other hand, is typically a salary you earn in exchange for work. Stop working, and the active income stops. That's why many people in retirement (or approaching it) end up relying solely on a state pension—because they haven't saved. Ask yourself now if a pension would be enough. If we have a source of passive income, in our case from rental properties, then as you build up your property portfolio, you should reach a point where you can decide if, and when, you want to stop working. The passive income stream is activated by the direct source of rental income from the properties. However, this doesn't mean a steady and secure income stream, as you will still need to manage the properties. So perhaps we should call it semi-passive. However, sell a property, and you will lose that passive income stream.

A simple example of passive income is from music royalties. The more a song is played, the more royalties the artist earns. That's right, each time a song is played on the radio the artist gets a royalty fee. No wonder Taylor Swift is so rich. If you really want to hit the jackpot, write a Christmas love song that is featured in a movie! One of the biggest earners of all time is 'The Christmas Song' (1944). Its estimated earnings are in the region of USD 19 million. But what are your chances of writing a hit song, or forming that profitable company? I don't rate mine too highly, so personally, I'll stick with property investing.

## 9 Long-term Rentals

There are many ways to invest in property. The best approach, in my opinion, is through long-term rental properties, and there's nothing wrong with starting small. These small properties can provide a solid foundation for future income. The properties require little, but disciplined, management, give great returns and should produce a positive cash flow for years to come. The buying, developing and selling of property is much more demanding, as it takes far more time, effort and money. Unlike rental properties, once you stop, the income stops. Rental properties have provided me with a continued source of income, and that's even without accounting for market appreciation, otherwise known as capital growth.

## 10 The 9–5 Job

When we start down our career paths, we often stay loyal to a company for years. It's often in the hope of working our way up the corporate ladder, with each rung offering greater remuneration. But that pay rise is often accompanied by more responsibilities and a heavier workload. We begin to feel irreplaceable to the company and become complacent because we fear change. Therefore, we stay.

My own career started at the tender age of 19. I got a lucky break when I was offered an internship with a major engineering company during the summer months. I worked hard, and I enjoyed the work and the challenges it presented. I honestly felt a real sense of achievement when I received my first pay cheque. However, in less than two weeks, I had spent it all. Sure, I had the latest stereo system and my friends certainly appreciated my new spending power, but I had nothing to show for it. I could probably be forgiven; after all, it was my first salary in the real world. The company kept me on, and as the weeks and months passed by, I would continue to earn and spend the money I had made. It seemed like a vicious circle, and each month I would tell myself that the following month I would begin to save. I didn't, not until one fateful day.

One day in September 1985 marked a significant moment in my life. So what was this defining moment? It was nothing more than learning from my parents' example and taking their advice. They had worked hard over the years, even taking an overseas posting to better our lives. I had two younger sisters and a much younger brother. We took family holidays, and life was good. They had even bought an investment property in Cyprus—Famagusta, to be exact. It would be a family holiday home. At least, that was the plan in the early seventies. However, in July 1974, Turkish forces invaded and captured approximately 40% of the island. From August 1974, the ceasefire line became the United Nations Buffer Zone in Cyprus, which is commonly referred to as the Green Line. Unfortunately, my parents' property was located right in the middle. Today, that part of Famagusta remains entirely sealed off by rusting barbed wire. Once a prime tourist area, it is now a ghost town and heavily guarded by soldiers. The forcefully worded signs make it clear that this is a no-go area. Understandably, my parents never invested overseas again. I cannot say I blame them. They still have a passion for property, but only on home soil. I think that this experience subconsciously made me more cautious when it comes to where I buy. Or, perhaps it's a case of knowing not to put all my eggs in one basket.

To this day, my parents remain warily optimistic that one day, justice will prevail and they will finally be compensated for their loss. For their sake, I hope so. If you are considering buying overseas, there are definitely some lessons to be learnt, but more on that later.

Perhaps the negative experience of the past was what prompted them when they told me to consider buying 'bricks and mortar' back in the UK. 'Should you ever lose your job, at least you will have a roof over your head', they said. They explained that getting into the property market at a young age would benefit me later in life. It meant that in 25 years, I would have the house paid for. 'But that's an eternity', I said. *Why don't I just start saving now and buy one outright later?* I thought. It immediately dawned on me that I never would. I wasn't disciplined enough. So I sat down with them and went through the payments on a property I could potentially afford. They gave me one more piece of advice: 'We can assure you of another thing', they said. 'Once the payments start, you'll probably forget you're making them; you'll be none the wiser, and you won't miss the money'. However, I did miss the money—well, at least to begin with. Or, perhaps I was just aware it was being taken from my account each month. But at least I didn't need to be disciplined, since the bank was doing that for me. Each month, the mortgage payment would leave my account and after a few months, I became none the wiser.

Why recall this story? Well, there's one element in property investing that affects us all, some more than others, and that's the element of time. Time really is of the essence, in more ways than one.

## 11  Time

Time is the only part of the equation that we can't alter. A recent survey by Post Office Mortgages indicates that the age at which the average prospective buyer expects to buy their first home in the UK is now 35. Compare this to 28 a decade ago and 30 only five years ago. According to the survey, in the early 1960s, the average age was 24. In France, the current age is 31. It is similar in the US, where the expected age ranges from 31 to 34.

Therefore, recent findings clearly show how much harder it is for those in their twenties to early thirties to afford a property. This is due to larger deposit requirements, higher house prices and stricter mortgage lending criteria than in previous generations. It's the same in many countries.

## 12  Getting a Foot on the Ladder

The above would certainly put many potential investors off. The obvious question being asked is 'How can I possibly get a foot on the property ladder, let alone build up a property portfolio, with statistics clearly indicating the difficulties?'

Well, help is at hand at many levels, certainly within Europe. The UK Budget of 2011 introduced a loan scheme offered by the government and house builders providing help to first-time buyers purchasing a newly built home.

Buyers needed to save a deposit that was equivalent to 5% of their property's value, with the government and house builders putting up 10% each through an equity loan. This enabled the first-time buyers to qualify for a 75% loan-to-value mortgage. The equity loan would be interest-free for the first five years, with interest charged at 1.75% in year six and at inflation plus 1% thereafter. France, on the other hand, offered tax incentives to those buying new properties.

If you are in your forties, fifties or even sixties, you may feel it's too late to build up a property portfolio. The good news is that pension regulations in the UK have changed since April 2015. They now allow people approaching the retirement age of 64 to use an unrestricted amount of their pension fund. Nevertheless, I would strongly advocate seeking financial and legal advice for anyone contemplating property investing in their retirement years to avoid taking undue risks.

Since the laws are constantly evolving, there is no 'right' time to buy. It will be down to you as an individual to decide when and how is best. That said, some periods are better to buy than others. I am referring to the property cycle, which we shall cover later.

## 13 Getting Started: Considerations

Getting started is perhaps the hardest part. One of the most commonly asked questions is 'How much do I need to invest?' There is no definitive answer. It will depend on the individual and their circumstances. However, deliberating on your current life stage and considering what is likely to happen in the coming years, at least in the next 5–10, should be part of the planning cycle. Consider the following:

- Marriage—Are you married or planning to marry?
- Separation—Are you recently separated, divorced or single?
- Starting a family—Do you have children? Are you planning to start a family?
- Education costs—Have you considered future university fees, accommodation and transportation.
- Health of parents—Will they need financial assistance or need re-housing?
- Redundancy—Have you evaluated your job skill set and job security risks?
- Chronic illness or death—What is the state of your health, do you have adequate insurance coverage?
- Your propensity—Can you make this happen?

Changes to any of the above would have an impact on your ability to get started. So it's not a question of one-size-fits-all. Instead, it's about understanding the limitations and budgeting accordingly. If you are in a stable position, then don't procrastinate. Remember, the sooner you start the better.

## 14 Start Sooner Rather than Later

At least in the UK, age is not the limiting factor on property investing, nor is it in many other parts of the world. In fact, what I am trying to emphasise is the importance of starting sooner rather than later.

When I bought my first property, I was working overseas in Abu Dhabi. Abu Dhabi is the capital of the United Arab Emirates (UAE), and, in the early eighties, freehold property ownership was available only to local Emiratis. Consequently, the only option was to rent. Fortunately, the company I worked for paid my rent. This gave me the initial funding from my salary to buy and mortgage a property in the UK, which was the only market I knew. It all happened rather quickly. I found, bought and signed for the property in June 1986. It was suddenly mine, and I felt immensely proud. I became a landlord. But at that time, I wasn't approaching the purchase from an investment point of view.

## 15 How Many Properties Should I Buy?

I am sometimes asked, 'How many properties should I buy?' This is usually followed by 'I know a friend with several properties, and he isn't rich'. Well, that's like asking 'How long is a piece of string?' The number of properties purchased by an individual will depend on the person and their financial circumstances. More importantly, it's not the number of properties you own that will define your passive income, it's the quality of the investments you make. One or two good investment properties will always outperform several bad ones.

There was an interesting survey done by HomeLet UK called the LandLord Survey of 2015. See Figure 1 below. It can be found here: **https://homelet.co.uk/homelet-rental-index/landlord-survey-2015** . This survey provided some key insights into the rental market and the tenant/landlord relationship. One particularly interesting segment was the number of properties owned by landlords. Here are the results:

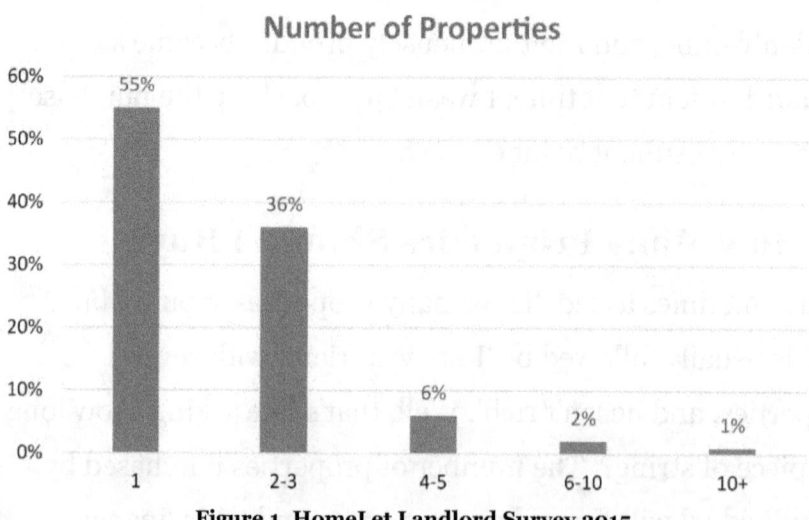

**Figure 1. HomeLet Landlord Survey 2015**

The survey shows that 55% only own one rental property. Thirty-six per cent own two or three properties, and only 1% own 10 or more properties. The reason for many landlords owning only one or two properties often comes down to either a lack of due diligence prior to the purchase or a poor understanding of the financials involved. Many understand that property is a great vehicle for passive income, so they buy a property or two 'hoping for', rather than calculating, the potential returns. They think it's a great investment if the rent covers the mortgage and taxes. 'The mortgage pays itself!' they say, but in reality, they haven't made adequate allowances for some of the most basic elements of property investing, such as repairs, voids and routine maintenance.

In some cases, they end up paying more each month to keep the property than they earn in rental income. It becomes a vicious cycle. The result is that many become disillusioned and sell.

I haven't compared these statistics to any other country, but I think they would be fairly similar.

## 16 Capital Appreciation

In general, property rents slowly rise and, over the years, so does the value of the property. This is true in most cases, but not all. These income-producing properties can provide a solid investment with a regular income stream. Over a period of time, often several years, they should also provide capital appreciation. Capital appreciation refers to the increase in the value of a property and takes into account any improvements made. As this principle is universally applicable to properties worldwide, I will use a fictional currency called 'Globals' (GBS) in many of the following hypothetical situations.

If a property was bought in 2010 for GBS 100,000 and is now worth GBS 150,000, the capital appreciation is GBS 50,000, or 50%. However, consider the following. First, that capital appreciation, or gain, as it sometimes called, is only realised when the property is sold. The second, and perhaps the most important (in my opinion), is that appreciation should be viewed as a bonus and not as part of the investment strategy. In other words, don't, as many people do, buy property on the assumption that it will increase in value. My business model requires the properties to be retained, not sold. Instead, we will use that capital appreciation for leverage. But more on leverage later.

## 17  Investment Strategy

So what is our investment strategy? At the most basic level, there are several ways to make money from a property, as I mentioned earlier, and they can be divided into categories. Market research and personal preference will play a major role, whilst demographics will also be a factor. However, no matter which country or countries you decide to start building your property portfolio, and ultimately your wealth, the fundamentals should remain the same. Here are the main types of property:

- **Residential**

This covers houses, apartments, condominiums, townhouses, holiday homes and student housing. Residential is the preferred choice for many first-time investors. A local rental or lease agreement is drawn up and signed by both parties. This determines the duration of the tenancy and amount that the individual or family must pay you.

- **Commercial**

This primarily consists of office buildings, high street shops and restaurants. Larger-scale business models include shopping malls or complete office towers. Businesses that occupy commercial real estate usually lease the space for an extended period, often several years. This ensures minimal business disruption. Rent is collected from each business that operates there. Businesses initially need location stability to grow, so, on the positive side, the chance of vacancy is reduced, as it can be very costly for a business to relocate. For example, if a restaurant has become established and popular, the owner(s) would be reluctant to move and lose its regular clientele. This is often offset by lower rental rates over the extended lease period. On a global basis, this is not always the norm. In Dubai, for example, the lease rates in popular malls are often negotiated on an annual basis. This is because demand for space often outstrips supply. It certainly keeps the business owners on their toes.

- **Industrial**

These properties can generally be broken down into three sizes: small, large and huge.

1. Small Industrial

Small industrial sites include single- or double-storey buildings specifically zoned for industrial use. These often have flexible interior space, usually a mix of warehouse and office space. They are often rented by start-up business. These units can carry a higher element of risk than larger businesses, which tend to be more established and therefore stable in terms of rental income.

2. Large Industrial.

Large industrial properties include medium to large warehouses and factories that are designed to manufacture or store goods. They often include distribution companies. In France, these are often located in the 'zone industrielle', which caters to this specific need.

3. Huge Industrial

On the larger end of the scale are the huge industrial spaces. These are often distribution centres for finished goods ready to be sent to customers. On this scale, it is often the company that owns the facility. Think of Amazon and IKEA.

Mixed Use Industrial

This is really a combination of the above. It allows you to diversify your investments, but unless you have deep pockets and several years' experience, I wouldn't suggest jumping in at the deep end just yet.

## 18 Which Type of Property to Start With?

I would have no hesitation in recommending that you start with residential property—not a holiday home, rather either a small house or apartment for long-term rental. If you already own a home, then you already have experience in finding, purchasing and maintaining a property. This means you're already one step ahead. Residential property generally requires less initial capital investment, and it's easier to understand and manage than some of the other types of property listed above, but the investment fundamentals are basically the same.

If you have only a relatively small amount of money to invest, you might want to consider investing in garages. They may seem unglamorous, but they are a great way to get started with minimal risk. Garage units are very low maintenance and, depending on location, relatively cheap to buy. It's true that the returns on one garage unit aren't great, but I have a good friend who owns a block of 12 that earn him a tidy sum every year. For the record, I don't own any, but I would consider them if the right location and number of units became available.

## 19 The First Step

Before you start looking at potential properties to buy, you first need to understand what you can and cannot afford. To do this, you need to get your finances in order. If you are fairly young, let's say mid-twenties, then you are probably employed and already earning a living. You are possibly residing in rented accommodation. If this is the case, then you already have regular monthly income and expenditure, but do you really know what those numbers are?

If you are older, the chances are you already own a house and have an existing mortgage, perhaps even a holiday home. Those in their later years probably own their house outright and are thus mortgage free. Regardless of which category you fall into, chances are you will need to take out a loan in the form of a mortgage through a bank or lender to buy your properties. These banks will most certainly look for an exceptional credit history and a current source of income. Lenders will often ask for three to six months' of recent income statements, and even more if the lender is not your regular bank. So building a spreadsheet to understand your finances will help considerably in both the short and long term. The short term is essential for analysing your current net worth and the long term for strategic planning.

## 20 Net Worth

Calculating your net worth involves subtracting your liabilities from your assets. If you have more assets than liabilities, you have a positive net worth. Conversely, if you have more liabilities than assets, you have a negative net worth. What defines an asset as opposed to a liability? In simple terms, they could be described as the following:

- An asset is something a company or individual owns.
- A liability is something a company or individual owes.

We can calculate net worth by making a simple spreadsheet to capture all these elements. Even if you think you have a good understanding of your income and expenditure, placing these numbers on a spreadsheet, like the one below, can help in many ways.

The table below (Figure 2) has been divided into assets and liabilities. The assets have been further divided into four categories, whilst the liabilities have been divided into two categories.

**Assets**
- **Liquid Assets -** An asset is said to be liquid if it is easy to sell or convert into cash without any loss in its value.
- **Investment Assets -** These are tangible or intangible items obtained for the production of additional income or held for speculation in anticipation of a future increase in value. These include stocks, bonds, retirement savings etc.
- **Personal Assets -** These are items of value you own, such as cars, jewellery, artwork, furniture etc.
- **Property Assets -** Often referred to as 'fixed assets', these include property, land, buildings and equipment.

**Liabilities**

- **Current Liabilities -** These are essentially bills that are due for payment within a short period of time. For a company, the debts or obligations are due within one year. These include rent, insurance, taxes etc.
- **Long-term Liabilities -** These liabilities extend beyond a year and include car loans, personal loans, mortgages etc.

### NET WORTH - GBS
Total Assets - Total Liabilities = Net Worth

| LIQUID ASSETS | |
|---|---|
| Cash In Hand | 3,920 |
| Checking Accounts | 2,500 |
| Savings Accounts | 400 |
| Other Liquid Assets | 100 |
| **TOTAL LIQUID ASSETS** | 6,920 |

| INVESTMENTS ASSETS | |
|---|---|
| Certificate of Deposit | 0 |
| Bonds | 12,500 |
| Stocks | 25,000 |
| Mutual Funds | 0 |
| Retirement Funds | 45,000 |
| Other Investments | 400 |
| **TOTAL INVESTMENTS** | 82,900 |

| PERSONAL ASSETS | |
|---|---|
| Vehicles | 36,000 |
| Home Furnishings | 19,670 |
| Jewelry | 16,600 |
| Artwork & Antiques | 25,000 |
| Electronics | 17,200 |
| Other Assets | 2,000 |
| **TOTAL PERSONAL** | 116,470 |

| PROPERTY ASSETS | |
|---|---|
| Primary Residence | 650,000 |
| Second Residence | 380,000 |
| Other Property | 0 |
| **TOTAL PROPERTY** | 1,030,000 |

| CURRENT LIABILITIES | |
|---|---|
| Utilities (per mth) | 760 |
| Rent ( per mth) | 0 |
| Insurance Premiums | 220 |
| Taxes | 220 |
| Medical & Dental Bills | 0 |
| Repair Bills | 125 |
| Credit Card Balances | 710 |
| Bank Line-of-Credit Balances | 0 |
| Other Current Liabilities | 180 |
| **TOTAL CURRENT LIABILITIES** | 2,215 |

| LONG-TERM LIABILITIES | |
|---|---|
| Primary Residence Mortgage | 320,000 |
| Second Residence Mortgage | 48,370 |
| Other Real Estate Mortgage | 0 |
| Auto Loan(s) | 36,000 |
| Appliance / Furniture Loans | 0 |
| Home Improvement Loans | 28,000 |
| Single-Payment Loans | 0 |
| Other Long-Term Loans | 0 |
| **TOTAL LT LIABILITIES** | 432,370 |

| | |
|---|---|
| **TOTAL ASSETS** | 1,236,290 |
| **TOTAL LIABILITIES** | 434,585 |
| **NET WORTH** | 801,705 |
| **LIQUIDITY RATIO** | 3.12 |

**Figure 2. Net Worth**

By adding up all our assets and subtracting all our liabilities, we arrive at our current net worth. In our example, this equates to GBS 1,236,290 − 434,585 = 801,705.

The line below 'Net Worth' shows a liquidity ratio of 3.12. So what does this tell us?

The basic liquidity ratio is a finance ratio that calculates the time (in months) in which a person can meet their expenses. It is calculated as liquid assets / current liabilities.

In the example above, we have current liquid assets of GBS 6,920 and monthly expenses of GBS 2,215. So 6,920 / 2,215 = 3.12.

Note: Liquid assets are anything that can be converted into cash in one day. So, if we had GBS 5,000 worth of stock that was going to mature the following day, we could include this sum in our calculation. In this case, the liquidity ratio would be revised as the following:

(6,920 + 5,000) / 2,215 = 5.38

Finance experts often recommend having enough liquid assets to cover expenses for three and a half months.

Using an online net worth calculator, or even creating your own, is a great way to understand the numbers. The important thing is to capture all the expenditure.

Whilst the above example shows a positive net worth and a good liquidity ratio, it doesn't tell the whole story, since it's only a snapshot of that day. To get a better understanding of our finances, we need a broader view. The earlier you start this exercise the better. Ideally, several months' worth of income versus expenditure should be captured. These data should then reveal a spending trend and, more importantly, reflect your financial stability.

| Budget Summary | January | February | March |
|---|---|---|---|
| Income (GBS) | 8,000 | 8,000 | 8,000 |
| Other Income (GBS) | 2,000 | 2,000 | 4,000 |
| Total | 10,000 | 10,000 | 12,000 |
| Living Expenses - Regular Repayment | 3,700 | 3,200 | 2,800 |
| Living Expenses - Utilities | 820 | 1,520 | 860 |
| Living Expenses - Occasional | 800 | 750 | 4,000 |
| Investment/Savings | 200 | 200 | 200 |
| Regular Repayment - Credit Card/Loan | 890 | 720 | 540 |
| Regular Repayment - Insurance | 300 | 300 | 300 |
| Other | 150 | 150 | 150 |
| Total | 6,860 | 6,840 | 8,850 |
| Income - Expenses | 3,140 | 3,160 | 3,150 |

**Figure 3. Budget Summary**

Whilst this spreadsheet (Figure 3) shows only the first quarter of a year, the summary provides a quick snapshot of income versus expenses. It's already a good indicator of eligibility to enter the market. In this example, we have an average of GBS 3,150 available at the end of each month. If your income came out considerably lower, let's say an average of GBS 2,000 per month, then it may mean that some lifestyle adjustments need to be made to raise the numbers. Fewer weekly restaurant visits perhaps? Or fewer shoes? While you are getting your finances in order, use your time wisely to carry out the search for property.

## 21  The Search

The search will often be determined by where you live. When I first moved to Amiens in France in the mid-nineties, I wanted to invest quickly, but I spent three months walking around the town just getting to know the streets and neighbourhood. This included the location of schools, parks, shopping centres and transport networks. Amiens is an hour by train from Paris. At the time, Amiens had a population of around 180,000; it was a large university town. I soon discovered the locations of the more desirable and affluent parts of town, and I also understood the rental market. Desirable does not mean either the most expensive or the cheapest. Desirable is the place where people wish to live and it is often related to the proximity of services and facilities, as mentioned above. You need to match the kind of property you can afford and want to buy to the locations in which people want to live. This might sound overly simplistic, but it's a very important aspect of successful property investing.

If I jump forward in time, I can take it a step further. A few years ago, I looked at investing in a rental property in Dubai Marina. I didn't need to spend three months walking around, as I was reasonably familiar with the area. What I concentrated on doing was narrowing down the proximity of facilities in relation to each other. I wanted easy access to a popular beach yet also be within a short walking distance to the local Dubai Marina Mall. I also wanted to know the proximity of hotels and public transportation. I knew a tram linking to the metro was going to be built, but I didn't know where the actual stations would be. After doing some research, I managed to find out the locations of each of the planned stations. This narrowed my property search considerably, and I soon found the property I was seeking. I knew the tram wouldn't be completed for a couple of years, but as I have said, property investing is long-term. I also knew that once the tram was complete, it would add value to the property. It all comes back to the most basic cliché in property—location, location, location.

## 22 Value Added Property

How much value does a nearby public transportation option add to a property? After looking at 41 studies of 15 rail systems, US researchers at California State–Fullerton concluded, 'Light rail transit has enhanced residential property values 2% to 18% in Portland, Sacramento, San Diego, and Santa Clara, with larger changes in cities with commuter rail systems'. In Dubai, the value is also variable but expected to climb, possibly reaching 10% in the coming years. On a property worth GBS 250,000, that's an increase of GBS 25,000—not bad for a few days of research. On the rental side, data analysed by a local newspaper found that rents in residential towers located near the metro stations opposite the marina in an area known as JLT were between 13 and 26% higher than those that were farther away. Therefore, close proximity to public transport reaching a city should always be a consideration.

## 23 The Deposit

We established earlier that with the help of a simple spreadsheet, we could reasonably track and calculate our income against our expenditure. Our income versus expenditure example gave us an average positive cash flow for the first three months of the year at GBS 3,150 per month. When buying property, we have another major advantage, and that's the fact that the full amount is not required upfront to make the purchase. If we look at it from a global perspective, in most countries your deposit would typically be anything from 10 to 40% of the property value. So if a property is for sale at GBS 100,000, the deposit could range from GBS 10,000 to GBS 40,000, rarely higher. This is based on the loan-to-value ratio, or LTV. If we saved GBS 3,150 per month for a full year, we would have GBS 37,800. That's almost 38% of the GBS 100,000 property's value, so we would be in a very strong position to qualify for a mortgage loan.

## 24 Loan-to-value (LTV)

The LTV ratio is a financial term used by banks and other lenders. It is the ratio of a loan to the total appraised value of an asset to be purchased. In our case, this asset is property. For example, if we wished to buy a property that had been valued at GBS 120,000, and assuming we could put GBS 20,000 from our own money as the down payment, then we would need to borrow GBS 100,000 (120,000 – 20,000). Therefore, the LTV would be calculated as GBS 100,000 / 120,000 = 0.83, or 83%. The remaining 17% is the GBS 20,000 we used as the down payment: 20,000 / 120,000 = 0.16, or 17%, rounded up. The higher the LTV ratio, the greater the risk to the lender.

For example:

- A loan of GBS 190,000 on a property worth 200,000: 190,000 / 200,000 = LTV 95%, High Risk
- A loan of GBS 175,000 on a property worth 200,000: 175,000 / 200,000 = LTV 87.5%, Medium Risk
- A loan of GBS 150,000 on a property worth 200,000: 150,000 / 100,000 = LTV 75%, Low Risk

For most financial institutions, the LTV threshold is 75%, meaning that your application is likely to be approved in the above example if you borrowed GBS 150,000 or less.

As a general rule, borrowers with a high LTV are considered higher risk by banks. In addition, the interest rates offered are sometimes higher with the possibility of supplementary terms and conditions applied to the loan. This is why it is important to build a good credit rating with the bank. Other factors will certainly be considered, such as your employment history, your income level and your expenditure levels, in some cases. If you already have loans or mortgages, the repayment history will be taken into consideration, especially any late or missed payments.

Even if you have a good credit rating, sometimes the LTV can be adjusted to meet the prevailing market conditions. In October 2013, the Central Bank of the UAE issued a new set of regulations. For expatriates, the Central Bank set the mortgage limit for the first property at 75% of the value for properties valued at AED five million or less. If the value of the property is more than AED five million, an expatriate could borrow a maximum of 65% of the value of the property. In the event of a second home or an investment property purchase by an expatriate, then the regulations state that the maximum loan available will be 60% of the value of the property. For example, a first property valued at AED 4,200,000 would require a mortgage of AED 3,150,000 based on an LTV of 75%. This means the down payment would be AED 4,200,000 − 3,150,000 = 1,050,000.

In essence, it would appear that the aim of the regulations made by the Central Bank was to regulate borrowing in the market by reducing the amount of leverage that was available to borrowers and increasing equity in property investments. Fast forward two years and the regulations have certainly cooled the market, but I can't help thinking that they have hurt many genuine buyers rather than punish the 'speculators' that caused many of the woes in late 2008/9.

## 25 Speculating

Buying and selling based purely on the expectation that the property value will increase is called 'speculating', and, whilst the returns can be exceptionally good, the investment strategy is very short term and often risky for both inexperienced and seasoned investors. Dubai made many 'speculator millionaires' in the lead-up to the crash of 2008/9. It also made many of those same millionaires bankrupt. Speculating has its place, but I am not a fan of this strategy. It's undeniably high risk, and with high risk comes high losses.

## 26 Buying Expensive Properties

As previously suggested, purchasing high-end properties (expensive ones) should also be considered a less favourable method of building a successful property portfolio, especially in the early years. It may seem desirable to buy a larger property on the assumption that it will bring a higher rent; however, the graphical representation is not linear. In many cases, less expensive properties may have more potential and yield better returns as long-term investments than the more expensive ones. Let's have a look at four properties, shown in Figure 4, to illustrate the point.

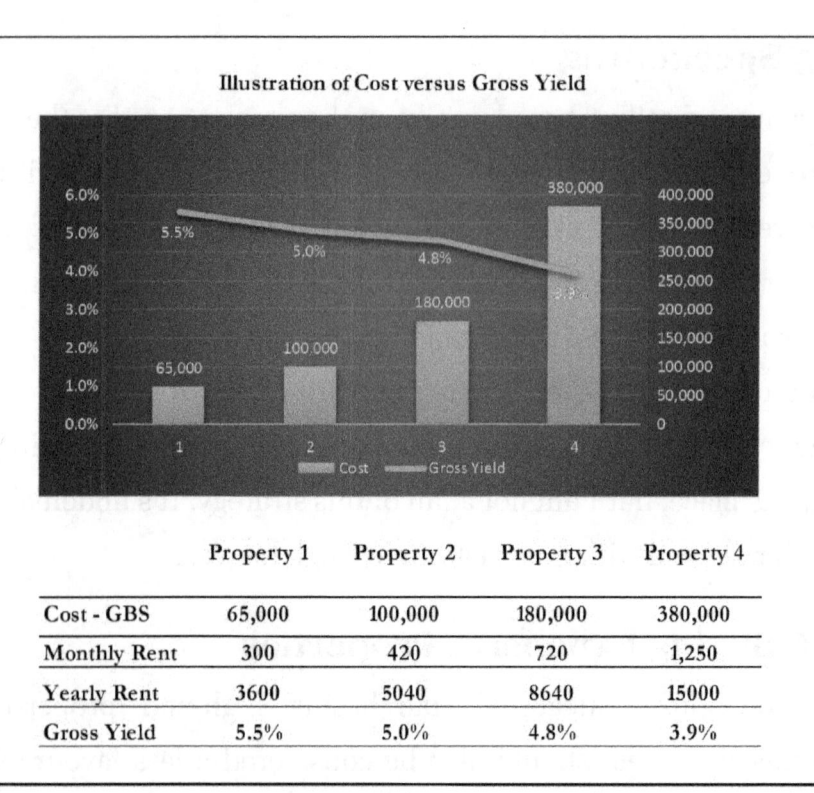

|              | Property 1 | Property 2 | Property 3 | Property 4 |
|--------------|------------|------------|------------|------------|
| Cost - GBS   | 65,000     | 100,000    | 180,000    | 380,000    |
| Monthly Rent | 300        | 420        | 720        | 1,250      |
| Yearly Rent  | 3600       | 5040       | 8640       | 15000      |
| Gross Yield  | 5.5%       | 5.0%       | 4.8%       | 3.9%       |

**Figure 4. Yields**

The above is based on gross yield, which is simply the annual rent divided by the property value. It is expressed as a percentage. Looking at the graph you can see that Property 1, purchased for GBS 65,000, would provide a gross yield of 5.5% compared to only 3.9% for the GBS 380,000 property. You need to take into account that the gross yield does not factor in your costs associated with the property in terms of its maintenance costs, property taxes and other expenses. You also need to account for income loss from vacancy. Vacancies, or property voids, are when the property is empty. These vacancy periods can last anywhere from a few days to a few months. They are typically the periods between finding new tenants. Another consideration is that the higher the value of the property, the fewer potential tenants. Remember, it's about affordability, not desirability.

## 27 Student Housing

Student housing is something I have only contemplated. However, it has now become a mainstream asset class. Some institutional investors specialise in student housing, regarding it as a safe and secure asset with relatively high yields. Whilst this form of investment has been prominent in the UK for several years, student housing is only now taking root in several other countries.

Higher education is fuelling the growth in this area. Many governments and local councils are actively driving the education sector, leading to an expansion of universities. The more universities, the higher the demand for accommodation. Most university campuses have limited accommodation facilities, so students often have no choice but to seek their own accommodation elsewhere. This is usually in the form of a 'house in multiple occupation', or an HMO. HMOs—let on a per-room basis to unrelated tenants—can be profitable but are high risk. All HMOs need a licence, and councils vary on the conditions required. In the UK, for example, renting a property to several individuals without permission could easily land you with a hefty fine.

If you are contemplating investing in student housing, then the key (which may seem obvious to many) is proximity. Of course, I am referring to the nearness of the accommodation in relation to the university. Generally, the closer the better. In some of the more educationally established cities in the world, savvy developers are building, selling and managing specially designed student accommodation, or student 'pods', as they are known. These pods, or studios, offer en-suite rooms in luxurious city centre buildings that are closely knit together and complete with gyms and cafés. It is a tempting investment opportunity and one I shall personally review. No matter how good the numbers look, remember that these investments are often sold 'off plan', so unless you really know the developer, you are taking two risks: the development risk and the management risk.

## 28 Debt-to-income Ratio

The debt-to-income ratio is another method used by banks to assess borrowing. It is currently set at 50% in Dubai and around 42% in the US. This ratio is used to compare income versus expenditure (debt). The lower the figure, the better your chances of getting an approval. The bank will compare your monthly debt against your gross monthly income. This debt-to-income ratio is now being introduced in the UK with some trepidation. For example, if your recurring monthly debt (that's your expenditure) is GBS 2,000 and your monthly income is GBS 6,000, your debt-to-income ratio is 33% (2000 / 6000 = 0.33, or 33%). However, if your monthly debt is GBS 3,500 and your monthly income is GBS 6,000, your debt-to-income ratio is now 58%, so you are unlikely to qualify (at least in Dubai) based on the current 50% guideline. Nonetheless, rules and regulations do change, so try to keep abreast of them.

## 29 Online Information

When I was seeking my first property, the internet didn't exist then as it does now in its current form. Nowadays, we have access to almost limitless online information. Deciphering what we need can be difficult. Whilst we can glean information about local purchases and rental rates for an area, it still doesn't provide the whole picture. I advocate that you speak with several local estate agents. Be specific about what you are seeking to gain as much information from them as possible. A good agent will certainly know which areas are popular and which are not. Try to learn why an area is or isn't popular. Moreover, they might know about any new developments, sometimes those that are still in the planning stage. These could include shopping centres, schools or even tram links, as I mentioned before. Always bear in mind that what may be perceived as a rundown area today could be the heart and soul of a town in the future.

I witnessed this transformation first-hand in Amiens, France, in 1999, in an area called St Leu. Houses aptly named 'Amienios' could be bought for as little as 18,000 francs each. These were typically two-bedroom properties with a small living room and kitchen downstairs and two bedrooms upstairs. In fact, they were ideal homes for young families and students. The river Somme runs right through the middle of St Leu, and the majestic Cathedral of Amiens is framed on the other bank. The town encouraged investment and offered incentives to try to bring the area back to life. A new university in close proximity was also in the planning stages. A few bars and restaurants were established, and today St Leu is one of the most popular tourist areas in Amiens, in the region of Picardy. It features numerous restaurants along the riverbank, and properties on the market sell in excess of EUR 200,000. That's an outright capital gain of EUR 185,000 without including the rental income you could have earned during the same period. Since the internet has its limitations, always speak with people.

## 30 Freehold versus Leasehold

When I bought my first property, I assumed I owned it outright. Luckily, I did, but there are two fundamentally different forms of legal ownership: freehold and leasehold.

When you buy property on a freehold basis, you own the land and building in perpetuity. You are ultimately free to sell them or leave them to your heirs. When you buy a leasehold property, you are buying the exclusive right to occupy a property for a set period. The period varies, but is typically 75, 99 or 120 years. Sometimes the leasehold period extends to 999 years. At the end of this period, depending on the terms of the lease, the property is returned to the landowner. So, if you bought a property that had a 99-year lease and 59 years had already passed, then you only have the right to use the property for 40 years before it reverts to the landowner. Generally, the shorter the lease, the less the property is worth.

For example, there are a large number of leasehold properties in and around London. If you are buying there, I would exercise caution, as some leases have less than a decade or two before they run out. Dubai also has a mix of freehold and leasehold properties, with the leasehold being for 99 years.

However, these properties are in the minority. Since the market is still in its infancy, the majority of these still have a good 90 years left, so investors are undeterred.

Depending on the country in which you buy, you aren't just buying a home. In essence, you are subscribing to a legal system that determines how you purchase and ultimately sell the property.

Some estate agents will evade highlighting the differences, especially as the leasehold period diminishes, but the difference can be a home that is worth buying and one that is not.

## 31  Exhibitions: A Source of Information

Whether you are a novice investor or a seasoned veteran, property exhibitions are another great source of information. They give developers the opportunity to display and create awareness about their projects, connecting directly with potential customers. You can source and discuss projects that meet both your budgetary and location requirements. At the same time, they present a great opportunity for investors to get an overview of what's happening in the market.

I have visited the Cityscape exhibition in Dubai over the past several years for many of the above reasons. Who really attends, and whom can you expect to meet?

Of course, we have the developers covering residential, office, commercial, retail, industrial, hotel and leisure properties. The majority, however, focus on residential.

The local authorities are also present, and these include investment promotion agencies, economic development authorities, city promotion agencies and authorities, location marketing agencies, regional development and investment zones.

The financial institutions are usually lurking in the wings, and these include banks, investment companies, pension funds, real estate investment trust (REIT)s, venture capitalists, insurance companies and fund and asset management companies, to name a few.

Finally, we have the all-important service providers that bring the projects together; these include architects, designers, urban planners, engineering consultants, major contractors, project management companies, real estate advisors and real estate solution providers.

As you can see, there is a wealth of information to tap, and it is all under one roof.

I attend exhibitions, because they often showcase future developments. This gives me real insight into up-and-coming areas for development. An exhibition can reveal the bigger picture, which is something I wouldn't get from talking to an individual developer. If you have ever been to Cityscape in Dubai or Abu Dhabi, you would know what I mean. I am sure it is similar in other large cities around the world. However, a word of caution: don't invest your hard-earned money based on a scale model of some future development. It's about the numbers, remember, not great models and enticing offers.

## 32 Stocks and Shares versus Property

A couple of years after buying my first property, I was approached by a financial advisor. I was still very naïve with regard to property and even more so when it came to investing in stocks and shares. The only advice I heard bandied about was to have a 'diversified portfolio'. After a few months of gentle persuasion, I bought a few shares. I diligently waited for my investment to grow as the months, and eventually years, went by, but it didn't. In fact, the share values slowly diminished. So, I cashed in what remained after a few years, lost some money and vowed never to buy shares again—and I didn't for almost 20 years. The second time around, I bought shares based solely on the premise that I would check their market value on a regular basis. I never did and the outcome was a mirror image of what happened 20 years prior. I haven't bought any stocks or shares since, and I don't intend to for the time being. However, I still occasionally receive phone calls from 'financial experts' offering me a plethora of investment opportunities. I remember one such recent call when a young man gave me his full sales pitch. I was in a particularly good mood that day, having just closed a deal, so I listened intently. Once he had finished, I recounted my history in detail to him and at the end (and without hesitation) he said, 'Look, you have had a couple of bad experiences, but it's just like going to a restaurant. Would you really consider never going to another restaurant because of a couple of bad experiences'? 'Yes', I said, 'I'll stay at home and cook for myself'.

You may get the impression that I am against buying stocks and shares and diversifying my portfolio. I am not, but what it really comes down to is personal preference and choice. According to research going back 100 years, despite all the crashes, buying stocks, reinvesting the dividends and holding them for long periods of time has been one of the greatest wealth creators. You would have done extremely well if you had bought Johnson & Johnson stock in 1944, or even

Microsoft in the early years. It's certainly easy to diversify stocks and using considerably low sums of money.

If you had GBS 20,000 to invest right now, you could buy a selection of different stocks across varying industries for a total value of GBS 20,000. Or, you could spend all GBS 20,000 on precious metals, such as gold. But that would be all you'd have, as that's all you can spend. However, that same amount could be used as a deposit for a house. We discussed LTV earlier, and regardless of whether you live in the US, Europe or the Middle East, the LTV threshold will vary to a degree. A typical LTV at present (and again, this will depend on your credit history) is 80%. So if we found a passive income property worth GBS 100,000, we could pay the deposit using the GBS 20,000 and finance the remaining GBS 80,000 with a mortgage.

- A loan of GBS 80,000 on a property worth GBS 100,000: 80,000 / 100,000 = LTV 80%.

I know I would rather have the house, and these are my main reasons:

- Buying in the right region or area can, to a degree, insulate you from a sudden downturn in the economy. Property in places like Paris, London, New York, Singapore and Dubai (to name a few) tend to hold their rental values. Stocks are far more volatile and fortunes can be lost literally at the stroke of a pen, or nowadays, with a few clicks of a mouse.

- With stocks and shares, you are effectively turning over the reins to another company or person and asking them to manage them on your behalf, just like I did. You become a minority investor; just one in the crowd. With property, you—and only you—are in control. All the decisions, from the rental rates you charge to the maintenance and running of the property, are down to you.

- Stocks are very volatile to market forces and the economy, which of course you cannot control. Property forces are much slower to react. This allows you to make important decisions with a degree of control and knowledge that directly affects your property.

- In some countries, there are tax advantages to owning property. This could be in the form of improvements or repairs to the property and even its long-term depreciation or the method of investing. They will vary from country to country, but these tax advantages should not be underestimated.

- We can calculate the returns when buying property with a good degree of accuracy. With some basic formulas and calculations, as I will shortly reveal, we can work out the income versus expenditure, and with an understanding of the market, we can even forecast several years into the future. This allows us to see if the property is a viable investment from the outset. To my knowledge, there is no such formula for stocks.

- Leveraging your property in a rising market is another way to build your property portfolio. It gives you a huge advantage over the more conservative cash investors. You cannot leverage stocks. By striking the correct balance between debt and equity, our net profits can be maximised. We shall cover leveraging shortly.

- Property, or real estate, is a physical asset. You can see it and touch it. We have always needed shelter, right from the earliest days of our ancestors, and we shall continue to need roofs over our heads. Since they don't make any more land, with perhaps a few exceptions (such as the Palm Dubai), property will always be an essential commodity.

- Each month when I check the rental income, I know my properties are working hard for me. Whenever I visit or drive by my properties, I feel my money is safe and that the calculated risks I took when I bought them are paying off every day.

- My main reason, however, is financial freedom that will one day secure my family's future and hopefully even be built upon.

## 33 Property Values: A Brief History

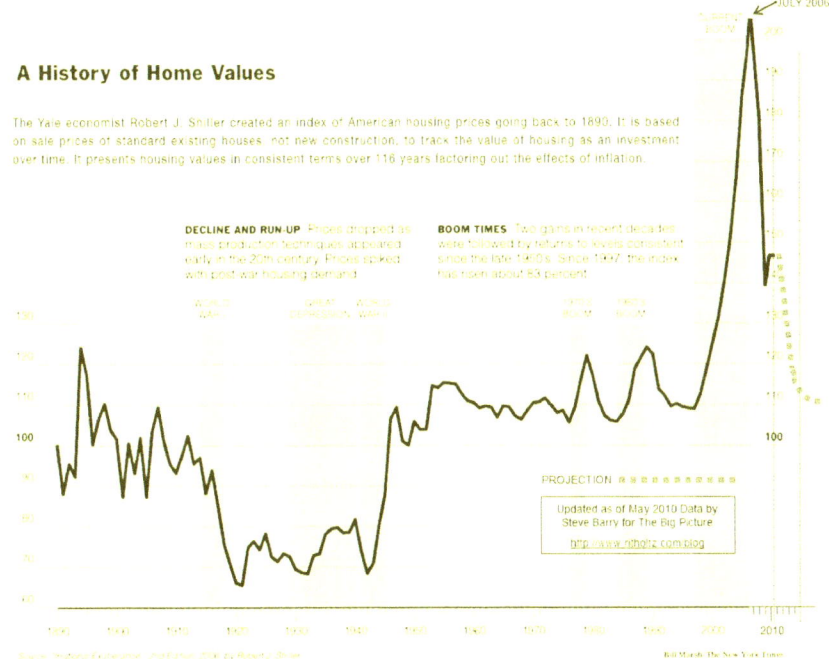

Figure 5. A Brief History of Home Values

In 2006, just as the Housing market was peaking, the New York Times ran this graphic (Figure 5 above) of the 100-year Case Shiller chart. It showed how radically overvalued

Housing had become. Two years later, Steve Barry updated that graphic, including the projected Home Price mean reversion. Whilst this is a US index of housing prices, the boom in mid-2005 was prevalent in many other countries as well. The financial crisis of 2008–09, also known as the global financial crisis, caused a massive price correction in property, as is evident from the chart. However, buying once the market had bottomed out would have been an optimum investment strategy. Predicting this period is the key, so research and trending information play a pivotal role in understanding past and future market trends. The chart below (Figure 6), from Credit Suisse, shows that the best performing house index is Australia, followed by the United Kingdom. It really illustrates that the global property market is perhaps more linked than many imagine. The trend is generally positive for all countries, reiterated by the average of the six countries shown in black.. The large price dive from mid-2007 in the US is very prominent. On the other hand, French property bought in the 1950s showed the highest price gain over the past 50 years.

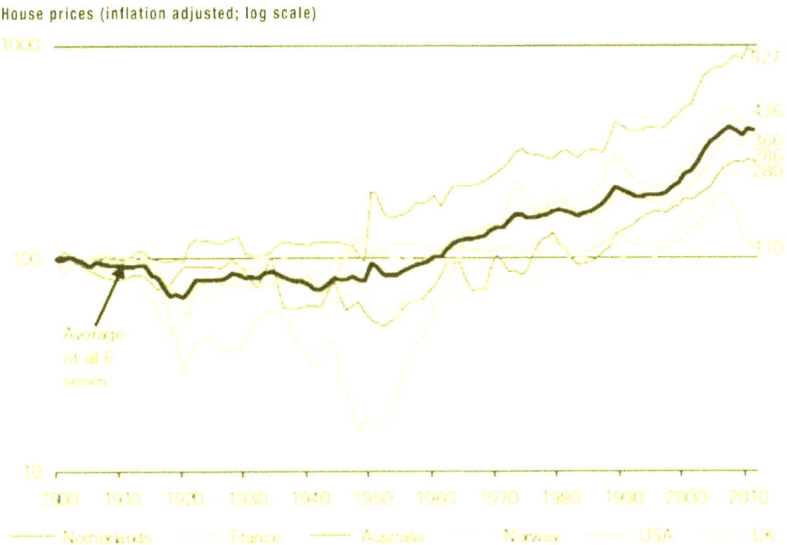

Figure 6. Domestic Housing Prices

## 34 The Property Cycle

It is widely recognised that property follows a predictable cycle. The property cycle has three recognised recurring phases: boom, slump and recovery. Buying in the right phase of the cycle is often key to optimising your return on investment.

**Boom**—during expansion and peak phases. Observations include:

- Rents rise, putting financial pressure on tenants.
- Property prices continue to rise.
- Property sales times are reduced from the time of being listed.
- Property finance is more readily available.
- Property speculation is rife with continued belief in market growth and capital appreciation.

**Slump**—following peak phase into contraction. Observations include:

- Reduced cash flow of investors
- Increased vacancies (voids) of rental property
- Property prices begin to fall
- Property sales times increase from the time of being listed.
- Property finance is less readily available.
- Property speculation has diminished significantly. Market sentiment is often negative.

**Recovery**—following the bottoming out of the market. Observations include:

- Rents begin to increase.
- Property prices begin to rise.
- Property inquiries (through agents) increase.

The property cycle, as graphically represented below (Figure 7), will undoubtedly continue. Predicting future housing prices is difficult, but the signs are often there. Some say that property values double every seven years, on average; for others, it is every nine or eleven years. The reality is that house prices are linked to inflation. In some countries, home values have not kept up with inflation, whilst in others; they have outpaced it and even appreciated in value. The key is to determine which areas are performing best, or at least keeping up with inflation. This leads to the question of when should you buy into the property cycle? For many veteran investors, the optimum period is at the bottom of the cycle. This is when house prices have crashed, and distressed sales loom on the horizon.

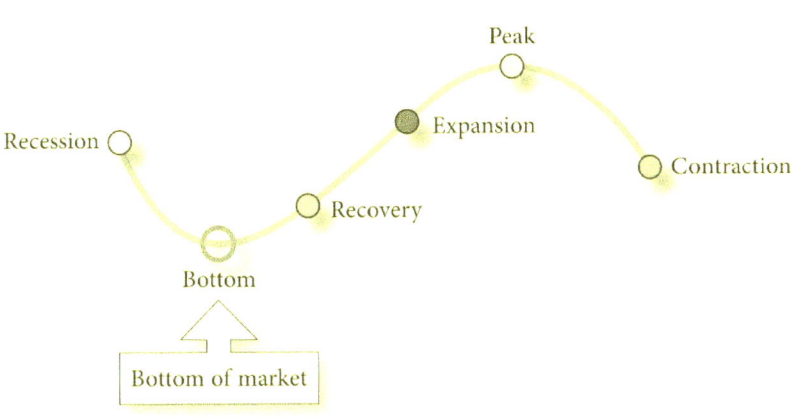

**Figure 7. An Economic View of the Property Cycle**

Geographical location is also important, as some areas will be more affected than others. The bottom line is that no matter when you buy your property, it must be profitable from the time of purchase. That said, if you bought a property at the peak and the economy waned, then the chances are that the property would no longer produce a positive rental income each month. Of course, rental prices can go down, so you should never count on appreciation alone since a peak period could be upon you without you being aware.

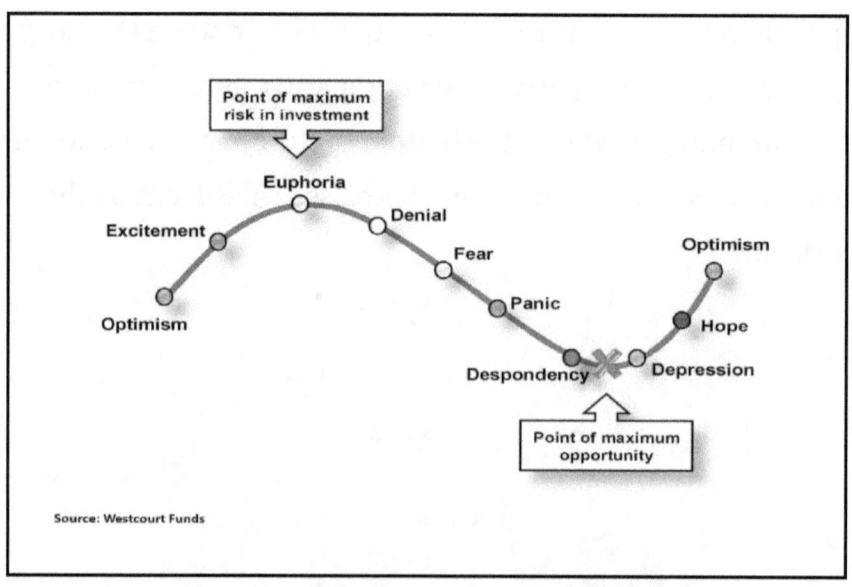

Figure 8. A Property Investor's View of the Property Cycle

Figure 8 above shows a property investor's view of the cycle. Buying at the peak means there is little chance of the property appreciating in value, but arriving at the peak is what we need to release equity. Therefore, when investing, you need to consider the stage of the property cycle. Remember that you would only sustain a loss if you sold the property at the wrong time, but we are not in the selling game.

## 35 Appreciation Creates Equity

Real estate, or property, appreciation is the increase in the value of your home. Property can appreciate in value for several reasons. London, Hong Kong and New York are obvious examples of places where building land has become scarce. Consequently, demand is high. Population and business growth are also major contributing factors along with location desirability. The addition of a new shopping centre, school or transport system can also boost pricing. The main factor affecting appreciation, however, is the state of the economy. If the economy is not doing well, housing prices may fall. For our model to work at optimal efficiency, we need a strong economy that leads to appreciation.

In the example below (Figure 9), if House A were bought for GBS 200,000 (as represented by the light blue area) and revalued two years later at GBS 220,000, then the appreciation would be GBS 20,000, or 10%.

However, don't confuse appreciation with equity.

**Appreciation -** An increase in the value of an asset over time.

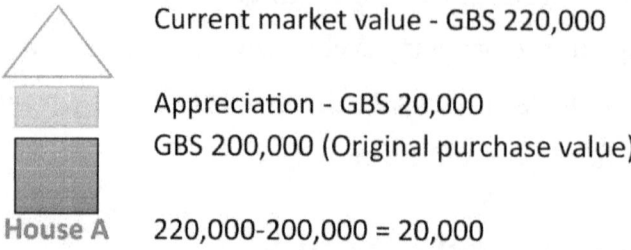

Current market value - GBS 220,000

Appreciation - GBS 20,000
GBS 200,000 (Original purchase value)

House A    220,000-200,000 = 20,000

**Equity -** The difference between the market value and the amount still owed. (Outstanding mortgage loan)

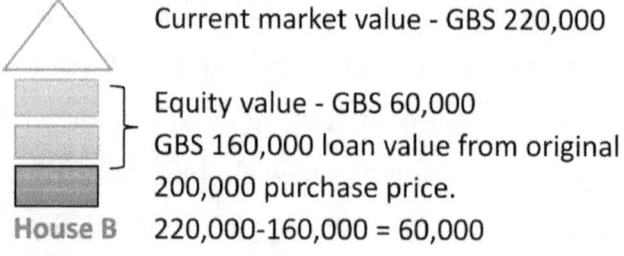

Current market value - GBS 220,000

Equity value - GBS 60,000
GBS 160,000 loan value from original 200,000 purchase price.

House B    220,000-160,000 = 60,000

**Figure 9. Comparison of Appreciation and Equity**

Let's look at an example of equity from House B, given above. It was originally bought for GBS 200,000. Using an LTV of 80%, we can work out the following: GBS 200,000 × 80% = 160,000 of the loan.

The down payment was the remaining 20%, or GBS 40,000, which was the original equity amount.

If we move forward three years, we see that the house has appreciated in value: it's now worth GBS 220,000. The GBS 20,000 of capital appreciation added to the down payment of GBS 40,000 would provide GBS 60,000 of total equity.

The actual picture is even better as you have also been paying off the debt (in terms of monthly mortgage payments); this could be an additional GBS 15,000, depending on the type of mortgage and term length. If equity is the difference between the value of the home and how much you owe the bank, let's readjust the equation:

The current value of the home is GBS 220,000 – 145,000 which is the original loan of (160,000 – 15,000 paid off), meaning there is now GBS 75,000 in equity.

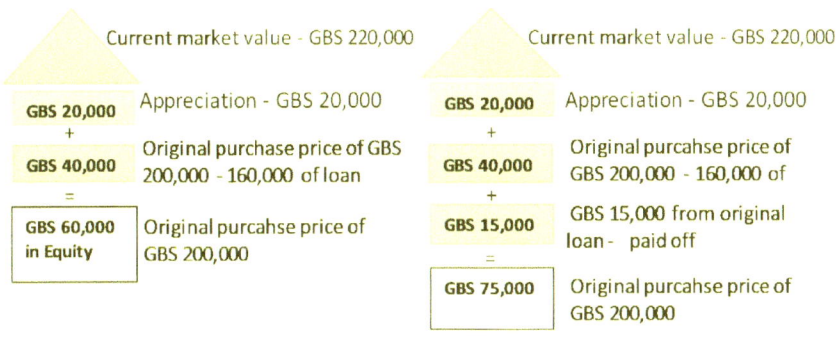

Figure 10. Comparison of Equity plus Principal from Loan Payment

The above example (Figure 10) shows how property equity is built. It is often a combination of capital appreciation and the principal paid down on the loan.

The best part about equity is that it can be used as security with a bank or lending institution against which you can borrow. Our objective is to use the equity to buy another investment property.

It is important to bear in mind that you can't use all of this available equity. Since the bank is lending you money against the value of your home, they won't lend you the full amount, hence the LTV.

Let's try the same example but extend the period to five years.

Your property was bought for GBS 200,000. A 20% down payment was made (GBS 40,000). The property market remained stagnant for the last two years, so the initial capital gain (appreciation) remained the same at GBS 220,000. Now, after a five-year period of owning the property, you are looking to refinance.

- Property current appraised value: GBS 220,000.
- Original mortgage: GBS 160,000.
- Current loan amount balance: GBS 128,000.

- Property value minus the current loan amount (220,000 – 128,000) = GBS 92,000 of equity.

Therefore, the additional two-year wait without any further appreciation of the property has still increased the equity.

The important element to this is how you use the equity, as illustrated in Figure 11. Let's take the GBS 92,000 of equity from the example above. If the LTV from the bank is set at 80%, how much equity could you use?

- 80% of 220,000 (current market value) = 176,000.
- 176,000 – 128,000 (outstanding loan amount) = 48,000.

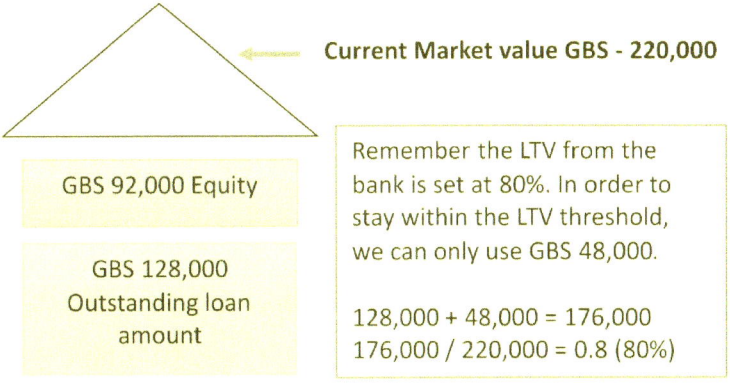

Figure 11. Equity

Let's say you plan to use the equity for a renovation project over a period of nine months. In this case, the best option would be to take a drawdown loan (Figure 12). As the loan is being progressively drawn down, interest and repayments will only be charged/calculated on the funds used. For example, if, by the third progressive payment, only GBS 16,200 has been drawn down on a GBS 48,000 loan, interest would only be charged on GBS 16,200.

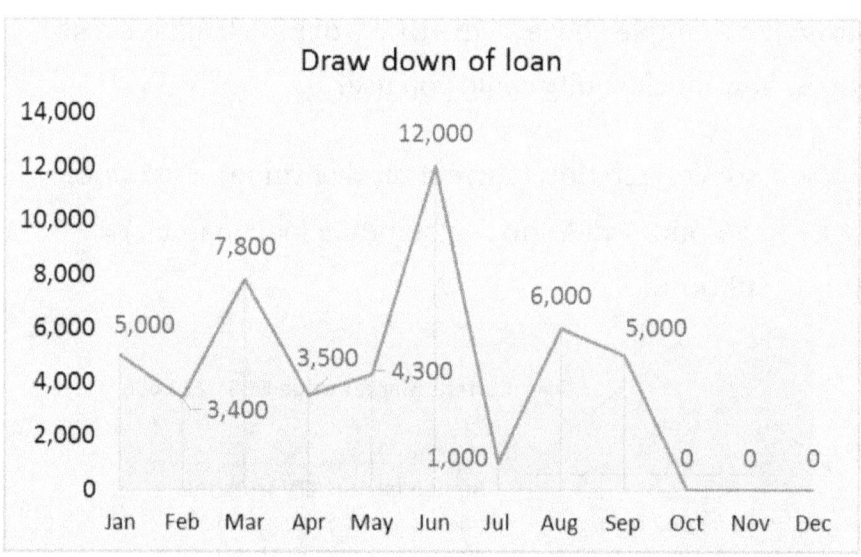

**Figure 12. Example of a Draw down Loan**

Many property investors, myself included, would be looking for a modest equity build-up that could be used to finance additional property. Releasing the available equity isn't a given right. Instead, you need to initiate steps with your local lender to ascertain the amount—if any—that the bank would be willing to release. The following is the minimum requirement set by most banks or lenders:

- Application form
- Valuation of the property
- Proof of ability to pay (credit rating; bank history)
- Fund usage (renovations, purchase of property etc.)

Based on the calculated equity amount, the bank would agree to the LTV. Let's consider two scenarios for an investment property:

**Scenario 1:** Cross-collateralised

- Market value: GBS 500,000
- Outstanding loan: GBS 300,000
- Equity: GBS 200,000 (500,000 – 300,000)
- LTV 80% (80% of 500,000 = 400,000)

Therefore, we could use only GBS 100,000 from the equity available. Assuming we use GBS 20,000 for costs and GBS 80,000 for the deposit, we could fund a house worth GBS 400,000 to stay within the LTV threshold, as shown in Figure 13.

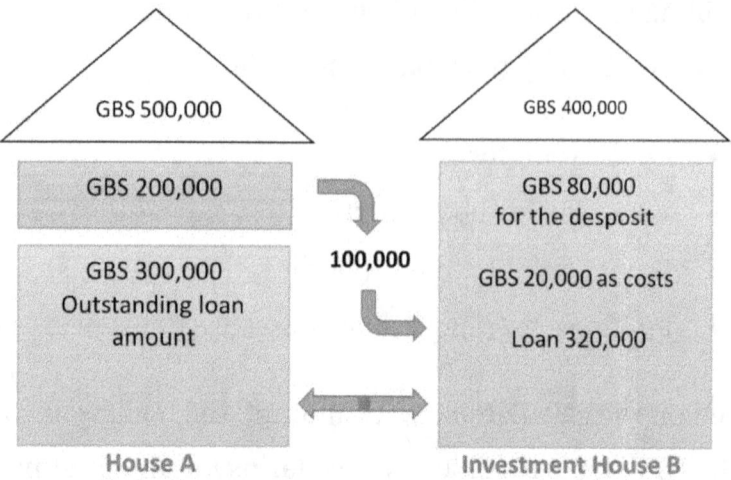

Figure 13. Equity Release for Added Investment

Once the second property is purchased, you would now have the following:

- Market value: GBS 900,000 (500,000 + 400,000)
- Outstanding loan: GBS 620,000 (300,000 + 320,000)
- 620,000 / 900,000 = 0.68, or an LTV of 68.88%, which remains under the 80% threshold.

In this scenario, it is important to understand the concept of cross-collateralisation. In relation to property, this means that one loan is used as collateral to secure another loan, often from the same bank. However, this puts you in a situation where your asset is still tied up with another loan when you pay one loan off.

The risk is escalated if your financial situation should suddenly take a turn for the worse. If you stop paying on one loan, your second property will also be at risk.

**Scenario 2:** Alternative Lender

- Market value: GBS 500,000
- Outstanding loan: GBS 300,000
- Equity: GBS 200,000 (500,000 – 300,000)
- LTV 80% (80% of 500,000 = 400,000)

As shown in the example below (Figure 14), we could use only GBS 100,000 from the equity available. Assuming we use GBS 20,000 for costs and GBS 80,000 for the deposit, we could fund a house worth GBS 400,000 to stay within the LTV threshold.

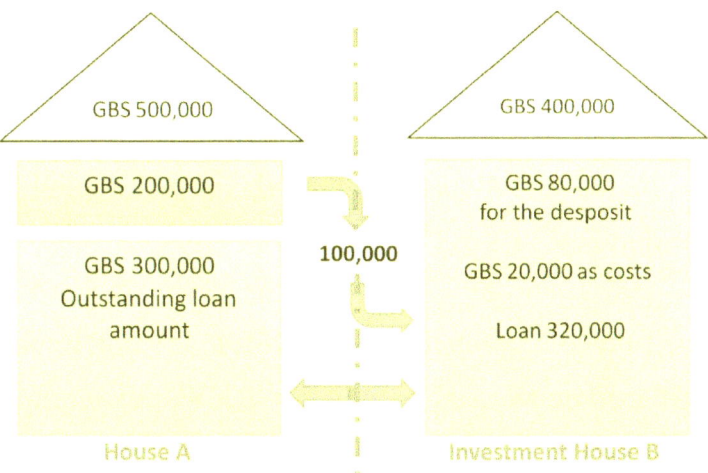

**Figure 14. Equity Release for Separate Investment**

Again, our market value, loan and threshold remain the same. The major difference in this scenario is that the loan is either separate or with another lender. It means the properties are not linked together. Should you default on one property, the bank or lender will have no lien on the other. If you have multiple properties, then I am sure that you can appreciate how spreading the risk is a wise decision to make.

## 36 Buying versus Long-term Renting

People are often torn between the choices of renting versus buying. Financial constraints and risk appetite are often key factors that lead many to rent, at least initially.

If you are embarking on an overseas assignment, either with or without your family, then renting for the first year would seem a prudent decision. By doing so, you can seek out the area that best suits your lifestyle needs either as an individual or family. This decision will invariably be based on local amenities, including schools, facilities and access to public transportation.

Regardless of whether you are going overseas or not, buying should be based on a longer-term approach. For example, if I were going to work in New York for two, or even three, years, knowing that I would eventually be returning to my country of residence means that I would probably just rent. However, if I were planning to live and work overseas for five years or more, then I would seriously consider the purchase option. This is certainly a dilemma for many in Dubai who initially came for a couple of years but now know they will stay longer.

Taking a simplistic approach, paying rent means that money is going to someone else—a wealthy landlord. At the end of your tenure, you will own no assets; you are not building wealth and will remain at the mercy of rental inflation.

Conversely, buying can build wealth, as we have demonstrated. Assuming market conditions are favourable, then inflation will actually work for you. It is a disciplined way to save money, providing both a tangible asset and the opportunity to build your net worth, grown through capital appreciation.

The above is applicable in most countries of the world. Yes, individual circumstances will always dictate the directions of some, but over a longer period, taking a pragmatic approach to buying should provide a more stable and financially rewarding future. In other words, buying allows you to become the landlord collecting the rent.

I remember talking to a couple of close friends over 18 years ago about buying a property. They live in Amiens, France. They had already been renting for several years, and so I delivered some impartial advice about the merits of buying versus renting. Even if it wasn't for investment purposes, I still wanted them to at least get on the first rung of the property ladder. I thought that once they owned a home then perhaps, just perhaps, they would realise the error of their ways and consider investing further. Alas, it was not to be. Their simple logic was that banks charge a lot of interest and they would rather save the money and buy a house mortgage-free. Fast forward to today, and they are still renting. They fell into the same trap that many people do: the inability to save. Whilst I am sure that they have some savings, I am also certain that they will never have enough to buy a property. Once they retire, they will have no other income and will still need to pay rent. All those years ago, they were worried about getting into debt by taking on a mortgage. Now, I think they have other worries ahead of them. Unfortunately, this story is all too common.

Let's assume for a moment that 18 years ago my friends had bought the two-bed 100 m² apartment that they are currently renting. Without accounting for inflation, we can make some simple financial assumptions based on the following:

- Property bought in 1998 for GBS 35,000 (seems cheap nowadays)
- Down payment of 20% (35,000 × 0.20) = GBS 7,000
- Mortgage loan of GBS 28,000 (35,000 – 7,000)
- Monthly payments based on a 20-year loan at 5% fixed rate = GBS 660
- Current market value as of 2015 is GBS 165,000

Remember that equity is the difference between the value of your home and how much you owe the bank, so GBS 165,000 – 4,212 (the current outstanding loan) = 160,788. Basically, if they sold the property today, they would have GBS 160,788 in hand.

Instead, they have rented for 18 years, paying an average monthly rent of GBS 750, which equates to a total of GBS 162,000 ([750 × 12 months] × 18 years).

Would you rather give away GBS 162,000 to someone else or have equity worth GBS 160,788 that's yours? As I said, their main worry was having less income by taking on a mortgage, thereby leading them into possible debt. There has been a lot written about debt. However, what we need to establish is the difference between good debt and bad debt.

So, is debt really that bad?

## 37 Good Debt versus Bad Debt

For many people, debt is a part of life. By definition, debt is the process of one party borrowing money from another party for a period of time. So, in essence, all debt is the same. We borrow now and give it back later. It is the consequence of this debt that really defines whether it is good or bad.

Good debt is used to buy something that either will increase in value or produce income sufficient to justify the debt. It can allow you to manage your finances more effectively and, with time, leverage your wealth.

But let's start with an example of bad debt.

Credit cards are an excellent example (yes, I have one, too). It is easy to put yourself into crippling debt by purchasing non-essential items on credit: a new living room suite, a new bedroom furniture set, the latest mobile phone, the latest and largest TV, an annual membership to a gym (you invariably know you won't use). The list goes on.

It's not so much the purchase, but rather the payments against the purchase that creates the bad debt. Many only make the minimum payment required, therefore carrying a balance on their account month after month. The interest payments then start mounting and payments are deferred. Unfortunately, this scenario is fairly common, and it's certainly a form of bad debt.

It is often said that bad debt is used to purchase goods or services that have no lasting value. However, occasionally buying the latest mobile or the latest and largest television may not have a huge individual impact, depending on your financial position. Collectively, however, it can all add up, leading to the amount you pay in interest, late fees, and any penalties to exceed the value of the product or service you have financed. Don't buy what you can't afford.

Some would argue that a car is an essential item. Therefore, it should be considered a good debt. Perhaps this is based on the assumption that the terms of the financing are favourable and that it will be used for business purposes. However, to my knowledge, a car depreciates in value the moment it leaves the showroom and continues to do so on a daily basis. I don't recall any car value increase cycles, with the exception of the wonderful classics. But we are not building a passive income stream from the collection of classic cars. Therefore, for me, cars are a bad debt. If you need a car at this stage, buy a used one and get it cheap.

Good debt, on the other hand, builds wealth. It's how you use debt that impacts whether it can be considered 'good' or 'bad'. If used properly, it can help us build wealth over time.

An example of this could be investing in yourself in the form of education. Whilst taking out a loan for further education is no guarantee of future wealth or success, gaining a higher educational qualification, such as a degree or even an MBA, is often associated with higher earnings potential. Many view the loan as a stepping stone, constituting a value that will pay for itself many times over.

By applying the same principles to a property, we essentially create 'good debt'. Let's be honest, most people can't afford to buy a home with cash, so we use financing in the form of a mortgage to pay back the loan over a period of time. In addition, the interest you pay on the mortgage is often tax deductible. We know that residential property can be an excellent source of rental income, as with many other types of real estate. We also have added the bonus of the property increasing in value. Whilst property prices can go up or down, historically over the long term they have tended to go up in value. This is true in the UK, the US, France, the UAE, Australia and many other countries. So, borrowing money to invest in this way can be considered a form of good debt.

## 38 Borrowing

Borrowing money for a property purchase generally comes in the form of a mortgage. Obtaining a mortgage used to be a case of meeting with the banker concerned in person and working through the finances. It still is, in some cases, but in others, this arrangement may be done through a broker. Either way, you need to be prepared in advance of the visit.

Here are some general steps to take:

- **Ensure your finances are in order**

Remember that banks or mortgage lenders are much more welcoming to applicants who have no other debts, since they are regarded as lower-risk borrowers. Banks used to offer mortgages based on a multiplication of your gross annual income; typically, this was three times your salary and two and a half times for joint salaries. Nowadays, it's more likely based on the criteria of affordability. In other words, your income versus expenditure is assessed. Therefore, having that all-important income versus expenditure statement prepared will both help your cause and demonstrate your financial acumen.

- **Savings**

As discussed previously, the banks or mortgage lenders will offer an LTV on the property you are looking to buy. For argument's sake, let's assume an LTV of 75%, meaning that on a property worth GBS 100,000, you will need a deposit of 25%, or GBS 25,000. That's quite a large sum for a modestly priced property. Depending on where the property is located, you will need at least 10% of the property value to put down as a deposit, often more. If you go to the bank with only 10% available, you may be rejected, so have a buffer amount ready. Remember, you have a better chance of securing a mortgage with a larger deposit. In addition, the greater the amount of the deposit you are offering the lender, the greater the access you will have to cheaper mortgage deals. The more deposit you pay, the lower risk for the bank, which in turn leads to cheaper mortgage deals for you. However, if you are just starting out, I wouldn't recommend buying in major cities, such as London, Paris or New York. They are prohibitively expensive and the yields are often very low. Many investors are seeking only the capital appreciation and have been known to leave the properties vacant. That's a dangerous strategy unless you have deep pockets. It means many young people in those cities are unable to get on the property ladder and end up commuting from further afield. Regardless of where you plan to buy, you will first need to save.

- **Record Keeping**

I have kept detailed financial records since I first started working—from bank statement to salary slips and even phone bills. Nowadays, I store most almost everything on my laptop (with a backup) in online folders for easy access. Having these records has proved invaluable on several occasions. Statements can be used to show a lender you have a consistent and reliable income, which in turn makes you a much more appealing prospect. If you are self-employed, use a reputable accountant to produce your reports.

- **Research**

Walking along the high street checking mortgage rates with banks and lenders can be time-consuming and misleading. Instead, there are many excellent websites that can provide instant and up-to-date comparisons between the major banks. This approach applies to first-time buyers and existing homeowners looking to switch deals. These sites also list the deposit required and associated fees and tie-ins. In some cases, the LTV is also listed. Figure 15 below shows an example from http://www.totallymoney.com/

| Provider | Initial monthly cost | Initial rate | Type of mortgage | Max LTV | Product fees | Overall cost for comparison |
|---|---|---|---|---|---|---|
| Chelsea Building Society Product details | £346.16 | 1.17% then 4.74% | Fixed for 2 years | 65% | Yes | 4.4%APRC representative |
| Yorkshire Building Society Product details | £346.16 | 1.17% then 4.74% | Fixed for 2 years | 65% | Yes | 4.4%APRC representative |
| TSB Product details | £346.98 | 1.19% then 3.74% | Tracker for 2 years | 60% | Yes | 3.5%APRC representative |
| Leeds Building Society Product details | £346.98 | 1.19% then 5.44% | Fixed for 2 years | 75% | Yes | 5%APRC representative |

**Figure 15. Example of Online Mortgage Deals**

Be aware that if you are refused a mortgage by a UK bank and then start applying to several other banks or lenders, you inadvertently create a 'Credit Trail' that becomes visible on your credit file. If you are rejected by four or five banks then the next bank will be even more reluctant as each rejection is visible. Instead, ask the lender to carry out a 'soft credit search' that will be recorded on your credit history but not visible to other lenders.

- **Mortgage Broker**

When securing a mortgage, you may be tempted to simply go to your high street bank—more out of convenience than anything. Instead, shopping around for the right mortgage can save you considerable sums of money in the long run, except it shouldn't be you who is doing the browsing. What you should be seeking is a mortgage broker who can help you secure the right financing for your property. More on brokers later.

## 39 Banks

When I bought my first house in the early eighties, community-style, branch banking was the established business model. There, you would deal with a branch manager or personal relationship manager. He or she was empowered to make decisions. A sense of loyalty was established. The manager and relationship managers became acquainted with you, forming trust. It all seemed to work. At the heart of the banking relationship was information.

If we fast forward to the present, the concept of branch banking has more or less disappeared. We have access to more information today, but we have shifted away from sitting in front of the branch manager to sitting in front of a computer and using online banking. Don't get me wrong, I do nearly all my banking online and find it convenient. For general banking needs, it works fine, but when it comes time to discuss mortgages and loans, the task should be done in person. Preparation has become key. You will inevitably end up talking to someone you have never met before. They will probably seem as though they should still be in school rather than deciding the fate of your mortgage application—at least that's how it is in my world. Therefore, having your income versus expenses spreadsheet prepared along with details of the property and a solid financial report is essential. If you are considering buy-to-let mortgages, the report should detail, at the very least, the following: return on investment (ROI) and vacancy, gross and net income. If these terms don't mean much to you, then they should. Any successful property investor should know not only these terms, but also the numbers, since the numbers really do matter. However, if you're not familiar with ROI, cash-on-cash or net income (along with a host of other calculations), don't worry. The good news is that we shall cover these in greater detail shortly.

## 40 More on Mortgage Brokers

There are many reasons to use a mortgage broker, but your main reason should be their level of expertise. Whilst cost is certainly a factor, their reputation is key and probably paramount to your success. A broker's reputation shouldn't be difficult to assess; in addition, a recommendation from a friend or family can be invaluable. In terms of the loans available, a lender that is 'fully independent' will have access to the greatest number. The majority of brokers charge either a flat fee or a percentage fee. In Dubai, I pay a flat fee. In the UK and France, it's often percentage based. It's also worth noting that most brokers receive a commission from the lender, so you do have some wiggle room for negotiation. Remember, this is a business transaction, so always negotiate. If you've ever been refused a mortgage in the past, or your credit rating has been a little sporadic, then a broker should be your first port of call, not the bank.

With one of my Dubai properties, I had planned to organise the mortgage myself. I was aware of the various interest rate offerings from most of the major banks at the time, but not the mortgage structure. I had just started the process when a friend suggested I use a conveyancing company to secure the best option. Conveyancing is the transfer of a legal title of property from one person to another, or the granting of an encumbrance, such as a mortgage or a lien. In other words, they help secure the best mortgage deal. The advice proved to be warranted. Whilst I consider myself reasonably well versed in most aspects of property, I am by no means a mortgage expert, nor do I wish to be. The broker managed to secure me an excellent rate with a bank that I had had no previous dealings with. Not only that, but the broker took care of all the formalities in a timely manner. When buying property, it's only natural to be more focused on the property itself than you are on studying the small print on the mortgage agreement. But the wrong mortgage can cost you much more than it should as well as incur penalties if you wish to switch providers.

As a result, in the past five years, I have started using a mortgage broker. I wish I had done so sooner. Dubai has a limited number of banks and a really limited number of mortgage options, even more so for the Islamic ones. The savings I made covered the cost of the broker's fee and reduced my interest payments over the long term. Consequently, I see it as a win-win.

In the UK, France and the US, the number of mortgage brokers are on the rise. Gone are the days when a quick chat with your local bank would secure a financial product as daunting and expensive as a mortgage. In my opinion, it's a change for the better. Even after a drastic cut following the financial crisis back in 2009, there are literally hundreds of mortgage options still available. A good mortgage broker is really worth their weight in gold, but what constitutes a 'good' broker?

The key elements are:
- Finding an independent broker with a broad selection of loans
- Transparent broker service charges

- Reputation
- Experience

It may be worth paying a little more for someone with a good reputation. If possible, have a face to face appointment with them rather than communicating by phone calls or email.

Ultimately, your finances must pass the stress test. In other words, you should save a little extra and create a financial buffer. Assumptions shouldn't be made. What is your contingency plan if rents were to fall by 5 or 10%? What if property prices fell by the same amount—could you still re-mortgage? If the property is left empty for several months, could you cover the ongoing mortgage, insurance and service costs?

That's why getting the right mortgage is the most important financial decision you will make. The more seasoned investors know what they are seeking in terms of the mortgage, and many will use a broker. For those of you that don't and see forgoing a broker as a cost saving measure, perhaps you should reconsider.

## 41 Mortgages

It's a very competitive market, so lenders and banks are continually updating and extending their range of mortgages.

The most important points to consider are how you will pay back the capital you borrow and the interest it accrues. Based on the type of mortgage, there are two main options for paying back the capital:

1. Pay a little at a time as you go (repayment mortgage); amortised
2. Pay it all off at the end (interest-only mortgages); non-amortised

- **Repayment mortgages**

This type of mortgage is very popular. Each monthly payment pays off a little of the underlying debt as well as interest on the loan. At the end of the mortgage term, typically over 25 years, the mortgage is cleared. It's perhaps the least risky type of mortgage and relatively easy to understand. These are known as amortised mortgages.

- **Interest-only mortgages**

With this type of mortgage, your monthly repayments cover only the interest on the amount you borrowed. The capital amount is not deducted from the original loan. So be warned, you should implement and maintain a suitable plan or strategy to pay off the capital at the end of the mortgage period. Interest-only mortgages certainly carry an element of risk. They are known as non-amortised or unamortised mortgages.

Interest-only mortgages have grown in popularity in recent years, especially in the UK, simply because they are cheaper than making payment on a repayment mortgage each month. However, you must remember that the principal amount will still need to be paid at the end of the mortgage period. This could be up to 30 years. If you took out a loan for GBS 100,000 today and had to pay it all back one year later, the inflationary value would have little impact. But, if you had to pay the amount back after 30 years, then the value would be worth far less. A simple analogy would be this: imagine buying your child a bike 30 years ago. Take that same amount of money and try to buy the equivalent bike today. You can't, but if you had to pay back the original amount for the bike after 30 years, it would seem like a bargain. This is due to inflation. Interest-only mortgages can work very favourably for long-term investments, especially if you have an understanding of inflationary and property cycles.

- **Buy-to-let mortgages**

Buy-to-let (BTL) are mortgages geared for landlords who buy property specifically to rent it out. To qualify for this type of mortgage, you will need compelling evidence that the rental income will exceed your mortgage, often in the range of 130% or more. So, if your mortgage repayment is GBS 1,000 per month, then the rental income should be GBS 1,300 or higher. You would also need to factor in vacancy. That's to say a calculated period during which the property may not be tenanted, due to a change of tenants, for example. Nowadays, banks and lenders are more cautious when it comes to the types of property they lend against, so invariably the deposit rates are higher—typically 25% or more. With recent changes in BTL mortgages, higher tax implications may also apply. This is yet another good reason to seek the advice of a broker.

I remember reading a very interesting article back in 2008 about a couple of teachers, Judith and Fergus Wilson. They had built up a huge portfolio of properties and became Britain's buy-to-let barons, with over 700 homes and an estimated fortune of 180 million pounds. The article failed to mention how they financed the properties, which were accrued over a relatively short period of around 12 years. It really came down to timing and risk. Research reveals that UK house prices have soared by 306% over the past 20 years. The combination of rising house prices, low interest-only mortgages and the ability to re-mortgage meant it was a prime time to buy, and buy they did. My personal opinion is that they went too far and lost focus. With the financial crash of 2009, the Wilsons exposed themselves to huge repayment debt simply by taking on so many interest-only loans. I can only compare it to a roller coaster ride. Despite warnings and media attention saying that it wasn't safe, they just didn't want to get off. They were having too much fun. They certainly saw the highs, and only time will tell how they dealt with the lows. As I said from the beginning, the best investment strategy is to create a level of passive income that meets your needs. It could be just a few properties that generate a modest income, to several hundred, like the Wilsons'. That leaves an awful lot of room in-between. Once you run the numbers, finding that happy medium should be evident, and it can then be moved up or down depending on your goals. But don't lose focus.

There is one more important aspect to mortgages, and that's the interest payments. You pay interest on most types of debt, and mortgages are no exception. The difference is the method of payment.

- **Variable rates**

This is a variable mortgage rate that changes whenever interest rates change. The interest rate changes are often calculated over a period of time, usually a year, and your payments are altered accordingly. So depending on the country's economic and financial condition, the market rates can either increase or decrease. Whilst you might not start with a variable mortgage, it is likely to change to a variable rate at some point.

- **Fixed rates**

The interest rate is fixed for an agreed period, usually between two and five years. Many banks and lenders offer an initial fixed rate to entice buyers. Whilst they are ideal for budgeting, you could end up paying more if interest rates fall, as you will be locked in at the higher rate. So having a good understanding of how the mortgage payment plan has been set up and any penalty clauses for early settlement or moving providers is essential.

- **Discounted rates**

A discounted rate mortgage provides you with a set discount off the lender's 'standard variable rate' for an agreed period, usually a couple of years. It provides lower initial monthly payments. The rate applied will fluctuate in line with changes in the variable rate, but it helps with the initial property acquisition.

- **Key facts documents**

UK mortgage providers are now legally bound to present customers with a key facts document. The Financial Services Authority (FSA), which regulates mortgages, says the key facts document should deliver clear, simple and user-friendly information to consumers about the mortgage offers. Each new mortgage customer has to confirm that they have received the key facts before putting pen to paper. Whether you decide to go with a broker or deal directly with the bank, you should at least be asking the following:

1. How much can I afford to borrow?
2. How can I tell which mortgage rate is best?
3. What is the best type of mortgage for me?
4. How should I repay it?
5. Can I make lump sum payments?
6. Are there any redemption penalties?
7. Does this mortgage come with insurance?
8. What other charges will I have to pay?
9. What happens if I can't pay?
10. What about the small print?
11. What loan period should I take?

Having covered net worth in an earlier chapter, you should be able to calculate the answer to question one. A good broker can provide the answers to questions two through eleven. You should discuss any aspects of question 10 that you don't fully understand with either your banker or broker. If you organise the mortgage yourself, then you should know the answers to all the questions. That's why it's important to understand the basic types of mortgages. In principle, it should be straightforward—you borrow money to buy a house and pay interest on the loan. But as you can now appreciate, it's not as straightforward as it seems.

## 42 Islamic Mortgages

The above are considered conventional-type mortgages; they come in many variants. But there are also Islamic mortgages available. I have used them myself in Dubai. They are starting to prove popular on a more global level. In Islam, making money from money by charging interest is not permitted. The underlying difference between Islamic mortgages and conventional ones is the way the Islamic mortgages are structured and how money is made. There are three models of home purchase plans (HPP), as they are called: Ijara, which means 'lease' in Arabic; Musharaka, which means 'partnership'; and Murabaha, meaning 'profit'. Depending on the model, the lender will levy rent or add profit to the amount you pay back instead of charging interest.

- **Ijara**

This is a lease-to-own type of mortgage. The bank purchases the property you want and then leases it out to you. At the end of the term, the bank transfers ownership of the property to you.

- **Musharaka**

This is a partnership type of mortgage. You buy the property jointly with your provider and gradually buy the bank out of it. For this reason, the mortgage is often referred to as 'diminishing'. If you put down 20% of the purchase price, the bank would pay the remaining 80%. Each month, you would pay the bank a monthly rent on the share you don't own in addition to buying more shares in the property.

- **Murabaha**

The buyer locates a property and agrees on a price with the vendor, as they would for an Ijara or Musharaka mortgage. The Islamic mortgage provider then purchases the property on their client's behalf. Once this property purchase has been completed, the financial institution sells the property to their client at a higher price, which is the cost plus agreed on profit.

Regardless of the type of financing you ultimately pursue, one recommendation when purchasing a property is ask for a 'subject to finance clause'. Your lender will want to value the property before they agree to give you finance, so this clause protects you in the event they don't agree with the purchase price and the deal falls through.

## 43 Principal and Interest

It is important to note that when you make payments on a 'traditional mortgage', you initially pay off more interest than the principal. But over time, the amount of principal being paid off increases, and so the equity after three years would not be proportional to the equity after five years.

| Months | Mortgage Balance | Payment Amount | Interest Amount | Principal | Ending Balance |
|---|---|---|---|---|---|
| 1 | 159,611 | 1,056 | 667 | 389 | 159,611 |
| 2 | 159,220 | 1,056 | 665 | 391 | 159,220 |
| 3 | 158,827 | 1,056 | 663 | 393 | 158,827 |
| 4 | 158,433 | 1,056 | 662 | 394 | 158,433 |
| 5 | 158,037 | 1,056 | 660 | 396 | 158,037 |
| 6 | 157,640 | 1,056 | 658 | 397 | 157,640 |
| 7 | 157,241 | 1,056 | 657 | 399 | 157,241 |
| 8 | 156,840 | 1,056 | 655 | 401 | 156,840 |
| 9 | 156,438 | 1,056 | 654 | 402 | 156,438 |
| 10 | 156,034 | 1,056 | 652 | 404 | 156,034 |
| 11 | 155,628 | 1,056 | 650 | 406 | 155,628 |
| 12 | 155,220 | 1,056 | 648 | 407 | 155,220 |
| Total | | 12,671 | 7,891 | 4,780 | |

Figure 16. Example Principal and Interest Payments

As you can see from the table in (Figure 16), we have been paying a mortgage amount of GBS 1,056 each month. This is the interest amount plus the principal. After 12 months we have paid a total of GBS 12,671, which is a combination of GBS 7,891 in interest and GBS 4,780 in principal. However, you should note that the ending balance is not a deduction of the amount you pay each month, but the principal only. So, in the second month, the principal amount of GBS 391 was deducted from GBS 59,611, giving an end balance of GBS 159,220.

## 44 Loan Pre-approval

Most homebuyers don't get a loan pre-approval before they start their property search. However, if you are serious about property investing, then getting that all-important pre-approval is a must. It's a competitive market, and having the approval in place could make the difference between winning and losing an investment property.

The documents for pre-approval are the same as if you were applying for a mortgage. The pre-approval will determine how much the lender is willing to lend you. At the same time, it will also determine your borrowing limit. It is not a loan obligation, and you can walk away at any point.

## 45 Refinancing

One of the biggest obstacles in property investing is securing funds for your deposit. This is generally true for the first property and subsequent ones. If you haven't managed to save enough, but you already have a property, then refinancing could be an option. However, certain criteria must be met to qualify. So what is refinancing?

It's basically the process of obtaining a new mortgage on an existing property. It's used as a means to reduce monthly payments, lower your interest rates and/or release cash from the equity that has built up. Whilst the prospect of reducing monthly payments is indeed favourable, most people looking to purchase additional properties use the refinance option to release the equity in their home. The equity is the difference between the outstanding mortgage amount and the current value of the property.

Assuming your property has increased in value, whether through capital growth, renovation or diligently paying off your mortgage, it's possible to use the increased equity as collateral to secure further financing.

**Example 1:**

Let's say you just purchased a rental property for GBS 250,000 and paid GBS 50,000 as the deposit. Your mortgage would, therefore, be GBS 200,000. Four years later, the value of your rental property has risen to GBS 300,000, and your outstanding mortgage debt is now down to GBS 160,000.

Assuming your bank or lender is willing to lend you 80% of the current property value, which, as stated, is now GBS 300,000, then the new mortgage would be GBS 240,000. After paying off the remainder of your old debt (GBS 160,000), you will end up with GBS 80,000 (less any expenses) in cash that you can reinvest.

The second reason to refinance is to achieve lower interest rates.

**Example 2:**

Let's say you took out a mortgage loan of GBS 100,000 at 7% interest to buy your rental property. The payments would be GBS 710 per month based on a 25-year mortgage. Five years later, you have paid off GBS 20,000 of the principal, and mortgage rates have fallen to 5%.
If you go for a mortgage refinance, you will be replacing your current mortgage with a new loan of GBS 80,000 at a 5%

interest rate. The payments would be GBS 663 per month based on a 20-year mortgage.

However, before you go back to your bank or lender for refinancing, consider switching lenders. The caveat, however, is that it needs to be worth your while, as the fees involved will be higher. That all-important broker could come in handy again.

So, refinancing can be used as a vehicle to release funds for an additional purchase (or even purchases) if the prevailing market conditions are right. Remember, the longer you own a property the more equity you generally build.

Therefore, it's all about timing and the transfer of risk. If equity is left in the property and the property starts declining in value, then you might not have the opportunity to refinance. You could even end up with negative equity, which occurs when the value of an asset used to secure a loan is less than the outstanding balance on the loan.

## 46 Mortgage Payments

One question that I am often asked is 'How can I calculate my mortgage payments?' It's a complex one to answer, because, as I explained, mortgages are calculated in different ways.

However, if we look at a traditional repayment mortgage, the calculation would be as follows:

The formula is: ***M = P [ i(1 + i)^n ] / [ (1 + i)^n − 1]***

The variables are as follows:

- *M* = monthly mortgage payment.
- *P* = the principal or the initial amount you borrowed.
- *i* = your monthly interest rate. Interest rates are often quoted as an annual figure, so divide it by 12 for each month of the year. If your interest rate is 4%, then the monthly rate will look like this: 0.04 / 12 = 0.00333.
- *n* = the number of payments, or rather the payment period, in months. If you take out a 20-year mortgage, this means *n* = 20 years × 12 months per year = 240 payments.

I agree it's not the simplest of calculations, especially when done on a napkin. The good news is that there are easier ways. If you are reasonably familiar with Microsoft Excel, then you will find a built-in function called PMT.

The syntax of the function is: **PMT( rate, nper, pv, [fv], [type] )**

Where the arguments are as follows:
- *rate* = the interest rate, per period.
- *nper* = the number of periods over which the loan or investment is to be paid.
- *pv* = the present value of the loan/investment.
- *[fv]* = an optional argument that specifies the future value of the loan/investment at the end of nper payments. If omitted, [fv] takes on the default value of 0.

- *Type* = an optional argument that defines whether the payment is made at the start or the end of the period.
  The type argument can have the value 0 or 1, meaning:
  *0—the payment is made at the end of the period.*
  *1—the payment is made at the beginning of the period.*

  o  If the type argument is omitted, it takes on the default value of 0 (denoting payments made at the end of the period).

## 47 Create Your Own Mortgage Calculator

Don't give up just yet. By creating a simple calculator based on the above, you should end up being able to calculate your monthly payment as shown below (Figure 17). I made this calculator using Microsoft Excel. Otherwise, there are several online guides to help you use the PMT function.

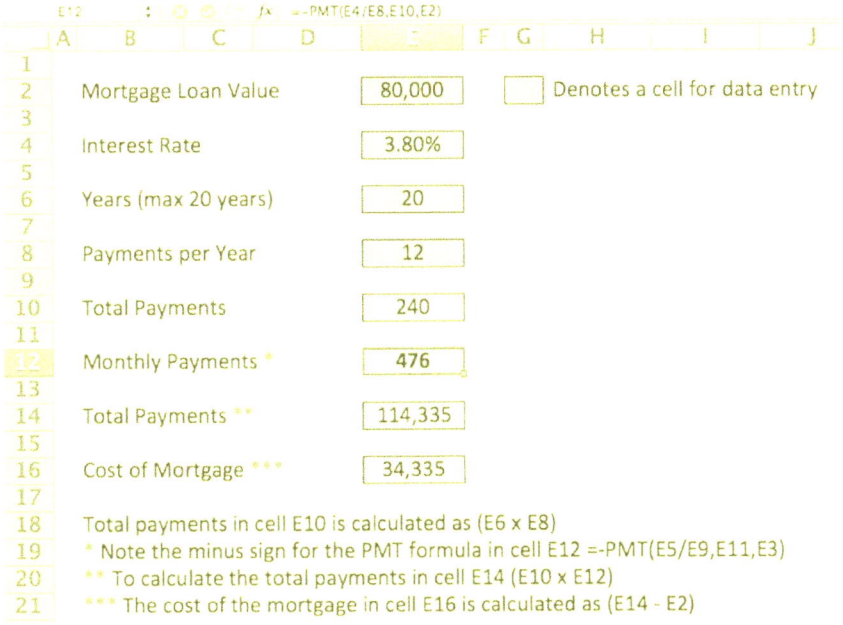

Figure 17. Create your own Mortgage Calculator

If you are not familiar with Microsoft Excel or spreadsheets, and the above is still confusing, then simply use an online mortgage calculator—there are literally thousands available. Just plug in the numbers, and it will do the calculation for you. However, it's not as fun as making your own.

As you can see, mortgages can become complex, and choosing the wrong one can become costly.

## 48 The 1% Rule

The simplest and quickest calculation of all is one called the 1% rule. All you need are two numbers: the price of the property and the monthly rental income. If the monthly income is at least 1% of the purchase price, then it's certainly worth investigating; some investors use an even higher percentage as the minimum. As an example of the 1% rule, if you have a property that costs GBS 200,000, and it rents for GBS 2,000 per month, then it's highly likely you will get positive cash flow from it. Positive cash flow, as we know, is the key ingredient to successful property investing.

The beauty of this calculation is that is works in any currency, including my fictional GBS. However, I don't use it myself, as I prefer a more in-depth approach from the start. That said, it's probably not a bad way to compare some initial properties during your preliminary search. You might even discover a surprise find. But don't forget that this basic calculation is only a rule of thumb. Obviously, the higher the ratio the better, all other things being equal.

## 49 Location

Something that I now advocate is investing in property that you have control over. That sounds fairly obvious, right? But let's go back to the first property I bought. As you may recall, I had just started working in Abu Dhabi. The property I bought was located in Bromley, UK. I honestly cannot recall why I bought there, but I paid £ 44,000 at the time and did nothing to improve the house. I hadn't really planned to rent it out and so it stayed empty for most of the time. Fast forward 18 months, and I had the property valued out of curiosity. It came in at £ 79,000. I was shocked. I thought this was the easiest money I had ever made. Of course, I made nothing in reality, because I hadn't sold it. That is when I made my first mistake.

Hindsight, as we all know, is a wonderful thing, but I didn't have it at the time. I knew very little about historical property prices or the impact of inflation. I sold the house for £ 78,000 and used a little over half as a deposit for a new house. I spent the rest. The house in question was being built in Horley, which is very close to Gatwick Airport. The price tag was a whopping £ 220,000. My plan at the time was unsurprisingly simple: rent the house once it was completed. I figured that if I had any problems, then due to its location, I could just 'fly in' and sort out any issues—not that I was expecting to have any. After all, I had the first property for 18 months and did nothing, so I didn't see why this should be any different. However, my intuition told me otherwise, because I walked down the high street and engaged a local real estate agency to manage the property and rental collections. As I recall, the monthly commission from the rent was around 10%.

The plan was to sell the property at a profit after a few years and use some of the money for a deposit and buy a bigger house—I figured I could have a house worth £ 1,000,000 within 10 years, but I figured wrong.

## 50 Don't Sell

My first mistake was selling the house. Building a property portfolio means owning houses—not selling one to buy another. I am not saying that you can't make money from buying and selling. Watch a few episodes of the popular British television series *Homes Under the Hammer* or the American series *Flip or Flop* and you will see that it takes time, money and plenty of effort. Sometimes the profits are very modest, sometimes large. But buy the wrong property and financial difficulties could soon set in. As the saying goes 'It's like throwing money down the drain, or in French ' Jeter l'argent par la fenêtre' (throw money out the window) You see its all property related.

Learn from the mistakes of others to build your property portfolio. Remember that this is a long-term investment, so don't rush into things.

Let's have a look at some of the common mistakes made by new property investors.

- **Buying the wrong type of property**

This is perhaps the most common mistake made by new property investors, as they are all too eager to own a property and unwilling to wait and ensure that they buy the right type of property. You first need to understand your target market. For example, are you looking to rent to students, young professionals or families? Are the room sizes suitable? Rooms too small won't attract families, a property too far away from the university won't attract students and a property with limited transport links might not be appealing to working professionals.

- **Location**

We have already covered the importance of location, such as the close proximity to schools or shops and transport links. The demographics of people living in the area could also prove invaluable. Properties in a great location are more likely to experience an increase in value, while poor locations are less likely to see major changes between each cycle. Furthermore, well-located homes are likely to have their high-value periods last longer than their unfortunately located counterparts. As nice as a property may be, buy in the wrong location and it won't rent, at least not profitably.

- **View the property as a business**

It's easy to say that your personal tastes and desires shouldn't come into play, but they often do. Let the numbers do the talking, and if they don't add up, move on and look for the next one. Don't overlook what other landlords in your area are doing. Find out how much they're charging for rent and how their properties are presented. Don't pass local estate agents' windows without viewing the adverts and summarising your findings.

- **Understand the rental market**

Not understanding the local rental market can be disastrous. Fortunately, this information is easily accessible on the internet. The facts and figures available can provide a wealth of information, such as rental trends over months or even decades. Analyse these trends for the area. Have they gone up or down, or have they been stagnant for many years? Remember, it's not a level playing field with some areas outperforming others. Again, this information is available, so use it to your advantage. Without looking into the facts and figures, you could buy a property that is not suitable for the local rental market. Study what the competition is doing.

- **Renovation costs**

Unless you buy a new property, then chances are it will need some degree of renovation work. New investors often underestimate the cost and time needed for this renovation work to be completed. Perhaps this is another good reason to watch an episode or two of *Homes Under the Hammer*. Misjudgement can lead to cash flow problems, and, invariably, short-cuts will be made to complete the work. Get the necessary quotes for the work, but leave a good buffer for any unforeseen work or delays.

- **Additional funds**

It's vital to have an 'emergency fund' set aside for each of your investment properties. This should be used for unforeseen repairs, such as a burst pipe or broken boiler. Without the emergency funds and with limited cash available, it could mean the difference between the work being done well and the work being done cheaply. Shoddy work leads to problems down the line and, more worryingly, angry tenants. So set aside a small percentage of your rental income each month to build the emergency fund.

- **Management**

Owning one property is certainly manageable. Surpass five and the challenges start to become evident—such as repairs, taxes and accounts, to name a few. Management depends on how close the properties are to each other but ultimately depends on your accessibility. Don't try to do all the management yourself. Slowly build yourself a team of reliable experts to outsource the work for you. It means that you can spend your time more productively. Professionals can often save you time and money, so you can look at them as another investment.

- **Making an offer**

Remember, your portfolio is a business, and the idea is to make a profit. In many parts of the world, haggling on prices is expected, and property should be no exception. Never be fooled into thinking you can't make a low offer. After all, you don't know the seller's position. Perhaps due to circumstances, they are after a quick sale. They can only say no, then it's back to negotiating.

- **Insurance**

Seek advice and shop around for insurance. Not having the right insurance could prove costly. If something major happens to the property, you need to be covered. Some policies will cover the loss of rental income or provide temporary accommodation to your tenants if your property is damaged and needs repairs. As with any insurance coverage, make sure you read the fine print so that you understand what's protected and what's not. The less you pay for coverage, the less protection you normally have. I also advise tenants to take out their own contents insurance as they often mistakenly believe that the landlord's insurance covers them. It most cases, it doesn't.

- **Overseas investing**

Don't be tempted by overseas rental properties unless you really have control of the management, as mentioned above. An apartment in southern France on the Cote d'Azur or a ski lodge in Austria may seem like a great investment during the peak season, but in the off-peak months, many are left empty, and that means no rental income.

I followed most of the above advice to the letter. What let me down was the management side. We've heard the old cliché time and time again: when buying property, think location, location, location. In my case, 3,000 miles, or 4,900 km, was too far to realistically manage my rental properties. I was checking on the rental payments only periodically and finally realised that the payment gaps were getting increasing wider. As it transpired, the agency I used was in deep financial trouble. They had collected the rent but deferred their payments to me. By the time I took them to court, they had already filed for bankruptcy. It was a costly mistake, and, because I was overseas, not one I could easily administer. At the same time, house prices crashed. However, I held on to the property and prices recovered, but it took over 10 years.

As I mentioned, hindsight is a wonderful thing. Had I kept the original property that I bought for £ 44,000 in Bromley, it would now be worth a little over £ 410,000 according to current market prices, with rental rates hovering around £ 1,150 and up per month. When I had it valued at £ 79,000, I should have re-mortgaged, released the equity and bought a similar rental property. If I had bought that one extra property back then, today I would have over £ 820,000 in equity (assuming the mortgage to be fully paid). More importantly, I would earn £ 2,300 in passive income each month. Start adding additional rental properties over the years, and you can begin to see how both equity and your passive income can climb.

## 51  Leveraging or Gearing

To build your property portfolio, you can use one of the greatest property vehicles available: it's called leveraging, or gearing. In simple terms, leveraging is an investment technique in which you use a small amount of your own money to make an investment of much greater value. If you had GBS 25,000 to spend right now, you could go online and buy GBS 25,000 worth of stock, not a penny or a GBS more. However, using that same GBS 25,000, we could get a loan from the bank with an LTV at 75% to the value of GBS 100,000. Property investing allows you to use leverage when you buy.

Leveraging needs to be done wisely and responsibly. When these criteria are met, you can often achieve a much higher ROI than you could without it. The properties should produce positive cash flow and grow in value over time. But, if you overleverage by stretching yourself too thin and taking out too large a loan, then you run the risk of not being able to support the property. If rental rates decrease, you may no longer produce a positive cash flow. This means you will need to support the mortgage from another source of income. If you can't support the payments, you may end up defaulting on your loan and perhaps even losing the property. This scenario is amplified if you own several properties financed in a similar nature. So, use leveraging to your advantage without overextending your resources.

Let's take a quick look at how leveraging can be used successfully in property investing to create that passive income.

Remember my friends in Amiens, France? I had talked to them 18 years ago about buying versus renting. They wanted to save each month until they had enough to buy a house loan-free. Well, let's suppose they had managed to save and had GBS 100,000 for an investment property. Let's look at a few options using Amiens, their hometown, for each of the property valuations using current market rates.

### Option 1. Buy an investment property with cash
- One-bed apartment bought for GBS 100,000
- Mortgage payments per month: GBS 0.00
- Rental income per month: GBS 570
- Annual gross potential income = GBS 6,840

## 52 Gross Potential Income

Gross Potential Income (GPI) is the total amount of money that is generated from rent during a certain period of time. Typically, the GPI, or gross scheduled income (GSI), as it is often called, is income portrayed on a monthly or annual basis. In the above example, the monthly rent of GBS 570 × 12 gives us the GPI. The GPI is calculated before any expenses associated with the property are subtracted.

## Option 2. Use leverage to buy two rental properties

- First one-bed apartment bought for GBS 100,000
- Deposit (down payment): GBS 50,000
- Mortgage payments per month: GBS 258 (repayment mortgage based on loan of GBS 50,000 at 3.80% interest over 25 years)
- Rental income per month: GBS 570
- Annual GPI = GBS 6,840 (see note above)
- Second one-bed apartment bought for GBS 100,000
- Deposit (down payment): GBS 50,000
- Mortgage payments per month: GBS 258 (repayment mortgage based on loan of GBS 50,000 at 3.80% interest over 25 years)
- Rental income per month: GBS 570
- Annual GPI = GBS 6,840

So, the annual GPI = GBS 6,840 × 2, or GBS 13,680, for both properties.

Total mortgage payments = 258 × 12 = 3096 × 2 = GBS 6,192 for both properties.

Subtracting the total GPI from the total mortgage payments would leave us with an annual gross income of GBS 7,488 (13,680 – 6192).

Therefore, by financing the purchases using a high 50% LTV, my friends would have been able to buy two properties. Those properties would have produced more income and increased their ROI. They would also have had the added bonus of capital appreciation on two properties.

If they had bought three properties based on the above criteria using an LTV of 33%, we would get the following:

Annual GPI = GBS 6,840 × 3, or GBS 20,520 for the three properties.

Total mortgage payments = 346 × 12 = 4,152 × 3 = GBS 12,456 for the three properties.

Subtracting the total annual GPI from the total mortgage payments would leave them with an annual gross income of GBS 8,064 (20,520 – 12,456).

There is another scenario to consider. What if they had leveraged and bought the largest house possible using an LTV of 75%?

- Four-bed house bought for GBS 400,000
- Deposit: GBS 100,000
- Mortgage payments per month: GBS 1,551 (repayment mortgage based on loan of GBS 300,000 at 3.80% interest over 25 years)
- Rental income per month: GBS 1,900
- Annual GPI = GBS 22,800

Subtracting the total annual GPI of GBS 22,800 from the total mortgage payments (1551 × 12 = 18,612) would leave them with an annual gross income of GBS 4,188 (22,800 –18,612).

As you can see, the largest property actually gives us the lowest return. Bigger is not always better—it's all about location, supply and demand. Amiens has very limited demand for high-end rental properties, unlike Paris. As a result, rental rates are considerably lower. However, this is offset by the price. What could you buy in Paris for GBS 400,000? So whilst it may be desirable to buy a larger property based on the assumption that it will bring a higher rent, in many cases the less expensive properties may have more potential as long-term investments.

Of course, this is not the whole picture. The above has been simplified to illustrate the power of leveraging.

Figure 18 shows the table summary:

| Option 1—One 1-bed | Option 2—Two 2-beds | Option 3—House |
|---|---|---|
| Cost—100,000 | Cost—200,000 | Cost—400,000 |
| Annual Mortgage—0 | Annual Mortgage—6,192 | Annual Mortgage—18,612 |
| Rent—570 | Rent—1,140 (570+570) | Rent—1,900 |
| Annual Income—6,840 | Annual Income—13,680 | Annual Income—22,800 |

**Figure 18. Table Summary**

As a landlord, or more specifically as a potential new landlord, one of your main concerns should be buying the property that will offer the best ROI. This is typically done by working out the yields. We have two types of yield: gross and net.

Rental yield is the amount of money a landlord receives in rent over one year, shown as a percentage of the amount of money invested in the property.

So using the three options in the table above, we can apply a simple formula to work out these yields. For the following examples, I have assumed 100% occupancy of the property.

## 53 Gross Rental Yields

Take the amount of annual rent collected and divide it by the total cost of the property. Multiply by 100 to get the percentage of gross rental yield (GRY), as shown in Figure 19.

| Option 1—One 1-bed | Option 2—Two 2-beds | Option 3—House |
|---|---|---|
| Cost—100,000 * | Cost—200,000 * | Cost—400,000 * |
| Annual Rent—6,840 | Annual Rent—13,680 | Annual Rent—22,800 |
| 6,840 / 100,000 = 0.0684 × 100 = 6.84% GRY | 13,680 / 200,000 = 0.0684 × 100 = 6.84% GRY | 22,800 / 400,000 = 0.057 × 100 = 5.70% GRY |

*Includes all costs, such as stamp duty, renovations and land department fees*

**Figure 19. Gross Rental Yield Examples**

GRY is probably the most commonly used calculation method for making an initial investment decision. It's the bottom line number to start with and pretty crude. It should be treated with caution, as it doesn't take into account your monthly operating costs. Use it as a rough guide only. A GRY yield of less than 8% is probably not worth considering, in my opinion.

## 54 Net Rental Yields

To calculate the net rental yield (NRY), subtract the annual expenses from the annual rent and divide this result by the total cost of the property. The result should be multiplied by 100 to give you a percentage for the NRY. This is a far more accurate calculation to help you determine whether or not the property is a good investment. The higher the yield, the better the investment opportunity, as shown in Figure 20.

| Option 1—One 1-bed | Option 2—Two 2-beds | Option 3—House |
|---|---|---|
| Cost—100,000 * | Cost—200,000 * | Cost—400,000 * |
| Annual Rent—6,840 | Annual Rent—13,680 | Annual Rent—22,800 |
| Annual Costs 600 ** | Annual Costs 900 ** | Annual Costs 700 ** |
| Rent minus Costs = 6,240 | Rent minus Costs = 12,780 | Rent minus Costs = 22,100 |
| 6,240 / 100,000 = 0.0624 | 12,780 / 200,000 = 0.0639 | 22,100 / 400,000 = 0.055 |
| × 100 = 6.24% NRY | × 100 = 6.39% NRY | × 100 = 5.50% NRY |

\* *Includes all costs, such as stamp duty, renovations and land department fees*

\*\* *Annual costs. Add up all the annual expenses, such as repair costs, insurance, taxes, agent fees etc. If the property is new, the budget for repair costs should be minimal, at least for a few years. The NRY takes into account the property expenses, although not the mortgage payments. If you are buying two properties at once, then often the combined negotiated and running costs are less.*

**Figure 20. Net Rental Yield Examples**

The NRY will certainly help you make an informed decision regarding the value of the property as either a good or bad investment. The obvious question then arises as to what constitutes a good rental yield. There is no definitive answer, as a multitude of factors need to be taken into consideration, not least the location. I personally wouldn't consider looking at anything with less than 6% NRY. Even then, the deciding factor would be the growth potential.

Let's remind ourselves again that this is a long-term strategy. Whilst the property may have a lower short-term return on rental income, it may well provide a higher long-term return on capital growth (equity), which can often give you a far greater earning potential opportunity. Remember, equity is the difference between the value of your home and how much you owe the bank. Let's fast forward 10 years and look at the same three properties (Figure 21). For simplicity's sake, we shall assume the properties have now doubled in value from the original purchase price and that half the mortgage loan has been paid off.

| Option 1—One 1-bed | Option 2—Two 2-beds | Option 3—House |
|---|---|---|
| Original Cost—100,000 | Original Cost—200,000 | Original Cost—400,000 |
| Market Price—200,000 | Market Price—400,000 | Market Price—800,000 |
| Outstanding Loan—0.0 | Outstanding Loan—50,000 | Outstanding Loan—150,000 |
| 200,000 – 0 | 400,000 – 50,000 | 800,000 – 150,000 |
| Equity = GBS 200,000 | Equity = GBS 350,000 | Equity = GBS 650,000 |

Figure 21. Property Values Doubled

Option 3 indicates the best performance in terms of capital growth. So, if the bank offered an LTV of 75% on each of the properties, you could have the following equity release:

Option 1—200,000 × 75% = GBS 150,000

Option 2—350,000 × 75% = GBS 262,500

Option 3—650,000 × 75% = GBS 487,500

However, if house prices dropped, or perhaps even halved, during the same period, then Option 3 would undoubtedly be causing you financial woes. In some cases, it might even lead to negative equity. Remember, this is when you owe the bank or mortgage company more than your house is worth. This affected many people in the UK in the early eighties, including me, and again had a global impact during the last financial crisis of 2009 when house prices took a steep fall. Negative equity is a problem when you want to sell your home. However, rents are not usually subject to the same dramatic price adjustment, so long-term rental investments should be able to ride this out. The simplistic example provided above certainly illustrates why it is prudent not to put all your eggs in one basket. In other words, spread the risk. If Option 2 were selected as our investment strategy, then the NRY would be higher for both properties. In addition, if one of the properties had a change of tenants, then you could experience a period of vacancy; this would mean no rental income. The second property, however, would at least cover some of these losses from its rental income. The type of property is driven by demand, but it is often the case that smaller properties offer the better option. Periods of vacancy can be spread, thus minimising losses.

## 55 Vacancy/Voids

This, as the name implies, is the period during which the property remains empty. It could be anything from a couple of days to several months. The aim of all property investors is to maximise the occupancy and minimise vacancy. Your calculations shouldn't be done without taking vacancy into account. The vacancy period is expressed as a percentage and will have a negative impact on your income stream.

For example, if we had a rental property that was generating GBS 5,000 per year but was empty for a month, then the vacancy would be 5,000 / 12, or GBS 417 in lost revenue. As a percentage, this equates to 8.3% of the total income. When buying an investment property, don't be naïve and think you won't have any vacancy periods—you will. If you buy student accommodation, for example, then you will have transient tenants. As the university year ends, you may end up with one or two months' vacancy before the next year's students take up residence. If you are renting to professionals, then the chances are high that they will move on after one or two years.

In Dubai, I experience less than 2% vacancy. Areas with very low vacancy rates, usually under 2%, are often called 'tight' rental markets. This is partly due to the high demand areas the properties are in but is also due to the fact that my rental rates are slightly lower than the market average. This has meant that I have kept tenants for an average of four years. I personally don't believe that renting is about squeezing the most rent out of your tenants, but some would argue otherwise.

During your property search, vacancy can help determine rental demand. Depending on your country of investment, a number of different bodies, including real estate institutes, supply property data that often include the vacancy rates. It is a statistic that is used as a measurement for the number of rental properties that are vacant, or empty. In essence, it denotes how many properties are untenanted at the time of counting.

The local vacancy data can be a useful analysis tool. A higher vacancy rate generally means a higher number of vacant properties. This, in turn, suggests you will have more difficulty trying to attract tenants. This is simply due to the higher number of rentals available on the market as competition.

A vacancy rate of around 4% generally indicates a fairly balanced market between landlords and renters—above 4% and renters tend to have greater power in negotiating cheaper rents. My properties in France hover around the 5% mark and have consistently done so for the past 10 years. As a consequence, retaining good tenants has always been a challenge.

As you can see, vacancy rates can vary, but they are a good indicator and should be deliberated carefully when considering an investment area. The rates don't often indicate the property type, be it a villa, studio or one-bed apartment, for example. So speak with local property managers or agents about any specific types of rentals that sit vacant.

In summary, the net rental yield is calculated as follows:

([Monthly rent − running costs] × 12) / (Property Cost + purchase costs)

Let's consider another example, as shown in Figure 22. It is broken down according to the cost elements and an assumed mortgage. The purchase price is GBS 100,000, and the monthly rent is GBS 670.

| Running | Monthly Cost | Purchase | Cost |
|---|---|---|---|
| Maintenance | 35 | Mortgage Valuation | 250 |
| Insurance | 12 | Solicitor's Fees (UK, France) | 600 |
| Services Charges | 10 | Stamp Duty (UK) | 0 |
| Agent's Fee 10% | 57 | Other | 0 |
| Vacancy 5% | 28 | Misc | 0 |
| **TOTAL** | 142 | **TOTAL** | 850 |

Figure 22. Net Yield Costs

Using the formula, we should end up with the following:

([670 − 142] × 12) / (100,000 + 850)

This equates to GBS 6,336 / 100,850 = 0.0628. Multiply the answer by 100 to get the percentage. In this case, it is 6.28%.

Depending on where you live and invest, the running and purchase cost calculations will vary according to local rules and regulations. Dubai doesn't have stamp duty, for example, but it does have land department charges that currently include a transfer and mortgage registration fee. These charges are applied when buying and selling a property and are regulated by the Dubai Land Department. In the US, however, you would typically pay 'closing costs'—these are all the fees and expenses associated with the closing or settlement of a real estate transaction, and they can vary dramatically, even from state to state.

## 56 Net Operating Income

In the US, property calculations are done slightly differently. The main calculation when looking at an investment property is the net operating income (NOI). This is the gross operating income minus the operating expenses. It is what you are left with once the vacancy and expenses have been deducted. It is important to note that just like the NRY calculation, the mortgage payments and depreciation are not included. Here's a working example (Figure 23) using our Option 1 numbers above.

| Terminology | Cost | Description | Calculation |
|---|---|---|---|
| Gross Scheduled Income (GSI) | 8,040 | This is the total anticipated annual rent excluding voids or vacancy | 670 × 12 |
| Less Vacancy 5% | 402 | Typically calculated from 3% to 8% | 8,040 × 5% |
| Gross Operating Income (GOI) | 7,638 | This is the GSI minus vacancy | 8,040 − 402 |
| Less Operating Expenses (OE) | 1,704 | Running Costs. Insurance, repairs, agency fees, service charges | 142 × 12 |
| Net Operating Income (NOI) | **5,934** | GOI minus the OE | 7,638 − 1,704 |

Figure 23. Net Operating Income

Property investment professionals use a number of financial tools to make their investment decisions. You shouldn't be any different. If you have the net operating income calculation, then you can take it a step further and work out the capitalisation rate (cap rate). The cap rate basically represents the estimated per cent return an investor might make on an all-cash purchase for a property. It can be used for estimating individual residential units or multiple commercial income properties. The cap rate represents the projected return for one year with the assumption of a cash purchase.

## 57 Capitalisation Rate

The capitalisation rate is a useful formula to know when looking at either commercial or rental property; however, it doesn't take into consideration the debt, the cost of the debt or cash flow. The cap rate is a percentage, usually ranging from 6% to 12%, which is used to determine the property's market value. Cap rate calculations use the current market value.

By knowing the actual income (or rent) that the property generates and then deducting operating expenses (not including debt costs), you will arrive at a property-level net operating income (or NOI). Once you determine the NOI, you simply divide that by the cost of the property (that's the price for which you are buying or selling the subject property).

The cap rate formula is: Operation Revenue – Operating Expense = NOI / Buying or Sale Price.

Here's a simple example based on the above NOI using a property price of GBS 100,000. The workings are as follows:

The property has an NOI of GBS 5,934 and a price of GBS 100,000.
5,934 / 100,000 = 0.059 (multiplied by 100 to give %)
= 5.90% cap rate.

Let's look at another example (Figure 24). Let's say you had an investment opportunity to buy three units of varying sizes. Each unit has a separate entrance, kitchen, bathroom and utility meter. In essence, each unit has the same amenities as a standard single-family home. The asking price is GBS 300,000

The units rent for GBS 1,000 (unit 1), GBS 900 (unit 2) and GBS 600 (Unit 3). The tenants pay the utility bills.

For working out the expenses, we can use 1% as a rule of thumb for the repair (maintenance) costs.

| | | | |
|---|---|---|---|
| Gross Scheduled Income GSI) | 30,000 | Total annual rent excluding vacancy | 1,000 + 900+ 600 × 12 |
| Less Vacancy 5% | 1,500 | Estimated | 30,000 × 5% |
| Gross Operating Income (GOI) | 28,500 | This is the GSI minus vacancy | 30,000 − 1,500 |
| Less Operating Expenses (OE) | 5,000 | Running Costs. Insurance, repairs, agency fees, service charges | 3,000 (1%) for repairs 2,000 (estimated). For greater accuracy always use known costs. |
| Net Operating Income (NOI) | 23,500 | GOI minus the OE | 28,500 − 5,000 |

Figure 24. Running Costs

Knowing the actual costs in previous years is far more beneficial than making assumptions. Be wary of taking a seller's word. Human nature often dictates that people will underestimate costs to make the deal look better than it really is, especially if they are trying to sell. Assuming we pay the full asking price, our cap rate would be the NOI / the value of the property.

GBS 23,500 / 300,000 = 0.078 (multiplied by 100 to give %) = 7.8% cap rate.

So what does this cap rate really tell us? Several things—first, remember that the cap rate comes from dividing the net operating income by the sale price. So, if the NOI increases, the cap rate would also increase. But, if the price of the property increases, the cap rate would decrease.

In the above example, with an asking price of GBS 300,000, what would our cap rate be if our NOI increased to 28,000? Let's see.

    28,000 / 300,000 = 0.093 (multiplied by 100 to give %) = 9.33% cap rate.

Let's use the original example again but assume that the price of the property has increased in price by 25% due to very high demand. What will happen to our cap rate?

    23,500 / 375,000 = 0.062 (multiplied by 100 to give %) = 6.26% cap rate.

Strong demand for the property has lowered our cap rate, but what defines a good cap rate?

A low cap rate of <5% often indicates strong demand. The property is often well-located, has low vacancy levels and a good rental yield. Prices in the area are high. This may also indicate that there is little room for improvement.

A cap rate in the 5 to 10% range would indicate average risk. The location is often commutable and the rental yield acceptable with average vacancy levels. This type of property has the potential for improvement.

A cap rate of >10% usually indicates high risk. The location is often poor, the rental yield low and vacancy levels high. It may have a high potential for improvement, but at the cost of high risk.

Each level offers a degree of investment risk, so sharing that risk across a balanced portfolio is probably the best method. However, unless you are a seasoned investor, you should be wary of a very high cap rate, especially for your initial property investments.

So what else can the cap rate provide? Here are its three main uses:

1. It is often used as a tool to compare potential investments in one area. Whilst the prices and income will vary from property to property, as we have seen, the cap rate can help determine which the better investment is.
2. It can be used to determine the investment payback period. In our example above, we had an investment property worth GBS 300,000 and a calculated cap rate of 7.8% (GBS 300,000 × 7.8% = GBS 23,400). Therefore, GBS 300,000 / GBS 23,400 = 12.8 years.
3. Finally, we can use the cap rate as a guide to pricing. If we know the cap rate for an area, it can be extrapolated to provide a guide to the property value. For example, if our calculated NOI was GBS 25,500 with a cap rate of 7.8%, then we can use the formula NOI / cap rate. Therefore, GBS 25,500 / 0.078 = GBS 326,923. An asking price below this figure would be worth considering.

The cap rate is only an indicative guide and is used more in commercial evaluations than individual investment opportunities. However, I honestly believe that understanding the different types of calculations can only enhance your ability to evaluate a good deal. The more often you carry out the calculations, the easier they become (honestly). You will also become more confident about knowing what a potential investment property is worth.

As I have said previously, understanding the numbers is really the key to making a good or bad investment. For those with a penchant for numbers, I recommend a book by Frank Gallinelli called *What Every Real Estate Investor Needs to Know About Cash Flow ... And 36 Other Key Financial Measures*. If you are looking for more in-depth explanations and working examples, then this book is a must-have.

## 58 The Tenants

Before we delve deeper into the types of calculations and how they can be used, we need to address one of the most important aspects of successful property investing: the tenants. The larger your property portfolio grows, the greater the chance that you will have bad tenants. It's an inevitable part of being a landlord. As your portfolio expands, you will need to either manage it yourself or use a reputable management company. As you may recall, I walked down the high street and engaged an agency to manage my initial property. The arrangement worked fine at first. I received my monthly statements, albeit they were a few months late. Please remember that back in the eighties, email was not the norm. As the months went by, the statements became more sporadic. When I did finally return to the UK, the agency had siphoned off nearly a year's rent and conveniently declared itself bankrupt. I really only had myself to blame. I had done no background checks on the agency nor had I done any due diligence. I learned my lesson. Despite the loss, the good news is that I still use agencies, but now I exercise much more caution.

Whether you manage the property yourself or use an agency, selecting the right tenant can make the difference between profit and loss, happiness and anguish. In most countries, including the UK, France and the US, the tenants pay on a monthly basis. In Dubai and several other Emirates, it is still common to collect the year's rent in advance. That's right, the whole year's rent upfront and in one cheque. Of course, some landlords do accept two or more cheques, but the rental amount is often higher.

## 59 Keeping Track of the Rentals

I have kept track of my own rental income ever since I was short-changed in the early days. I have had fun building spreadsheets and graphs showing my rental income over the years. I continue to do so, but it's been a personal choice. I have no doubt that there are many excellent software packages that offer untold analysis and tracking options. Perhaps one day I shall succumb and use one. Be warned, however, that the complexity of some of these software packages can be counterproductive. Don't buy an all-encompassing software package that includes commercial real estate if you never plan to use it. You can review most products online before purchasing them, and some even have a free trial period. Keep it simple. My advice is to keep a close eye on all your expenses, not just the rental income, especially for your initial properties. Use a basic spreadsheet or a software package that meets your needs. This will really build your understanding of the running costs. It's also why I would advocate buying a relatively new property to begin with (new being no more than five years old). That way, any teething problems should have already been sorted. The last thing you want from an older property is unforeseen repair costs.

## 60 Tenancy Contracts

Tenancy contracts will vary from country to country, but in essence, they cover the main terms and conditions during the rental period. If you do decide to find tenants by yourself, then you have plenty of media options available.

Advertising in the local paper is an obvious one. Some papers offer free classifieds, but the downside is you are given limited space, so the description needs to be precise and accurate. You should at least be mentioning the location, number of bedrooms and bathrooms along with parking (if available) and of course the expected rent. If you want to reach a wider audience, then an online portal specialising in property is certainly recommended. In France, I often use www.leboncoin.fr. In the UK I would recommend www.rightmove.co.uk and in Dubai, I typically use www.propertyfinder.ae or www.justrentals.com. Of course, there are many good sites available, so it's really down to your own preference, but I will offer one piece of valuable advice. Most of these online sites allow you to upload photos of the property, so please don't use shots of dirty dishes on the sink or clothes scattered across a bedroom. 'A picture is worth a thousand words'—enough said.

## 61 Viewings

Prior to receiving an inquiry, it is a good idea to imagine the roles reversed. In other words, if you were the prospective tenant, what questions would you ask? The obvious ones would relate to the running costs, such as the monthly utility bills (water, gas and electric). Other questions may relate to nearby amenities and local transportation connections. Room size is another. Many prospective tenants will often already have furniture, so they will want to ensure that it will fit. Having the dimensions in both square feet ($ft^2$) and meters square ($m^2$) at hand is really important. Some of the less obvious questions are: 'Is the property pet-friendly?' 'Does it have double glazing?' I have even been asked about the building orientation on a few occasions. Many prospective tenants want to ensure that the main living room captures the maximum sunlight. So having these facts readily available is always appreciated.

The actual viewing should be coordinated—have the property open and available for inspection at a specific time, usually late afternoon. A window of a couple of hours should be more than sufficient. Introduce yourself and welcome the prospective tenants inside. Invite them to look around, and if they have any questions, tell them to feel free to ask. Let them inspect the property unrestricted.

Those that are genuinely interested will often show it; others will simply say thank you and leave. Either way, you should ask for their contact details. If you are offered a deposit, reply positively but tell them you will review their application. At this stage, you should also request references. You should get back to them with 24 to 48 hours. During this period, you will need to contact their references, which may include their employer. If, on the other hand, you use an agency, then all the above is their undertaking.

When it comes to the tenancy application form, there is no set standard, but there are standard terms and conditions. These include, but are not limited to, the following:

- The names of all parties involved (landlord[s] and tenant[s])
- The rental price and payment method (monthly, standing order, other)
- The deposit amount (usually one month's rent)
- Rent review period (usually annual or bi-annual)
- The start and end dates of the tenancy contract
- The property address
- Tenant and landlord obligations
- Minor repair and maintenance responsibilities
- Responsibilities of bills (utilities)

It should also include information on:

- Whether the tenancy can be terminated early
- Whether the property can be sublet to someone else
- Whether pets are allowed
- Smoking policy

I also include a clause stating that the tenants are responsible for taking out home contents insurance. In the unlikely event that something goes wrong within the property (a burst water heater springs to mind), then the last thing you need to be worrying about is the replacement cost should any of their goods get damaged. When all is said and done, the terms of the tenancy contract must be fair and comply with the law.

A good tenant is not necessarily the one with the most money. I once had a judge rent one of my properties. Whilst the rent was always paid on time, the property wasn't looked after. At the end of the rental period, which was three years, the deposit was forfeited without question. What's the saying? 'Never judge a book by its cover'. Consequently, references are extremely important. If the tenants are a couple, you should be asking questions such as do they both have jobs? Have they rented before? If so, are they happy for you to check with their previous landlord? A no to the last question should raise concerns. You can probably appreciate now why I prefer to use an agency. The last piece of advice when looking for tenants is that you shouldn't rent to family or friends. I have broken this rule several times, but repairs, damage and rent increases (among others) become awkward to negotiate with people you know well.

## 62 Breakeven

Tenants play a critical role, so understanding the breakeven occupancy ratio of a potential investment is a handy tool. The breakeven occupancy ratio is simply the sum of all operating expenses and debt service divided by the total potential rental income. The vacancy period is not included. This tells you what percentage of the property must be rented out to cover all expenses and debt service obligations.

The breakeven ratio is easy to calculate and should definitely be included as part of your calculation toolbox. When negotiating a purchase, it could provide a degree of leverage, especially if the vacancy rates have been on the high side. It can also provide a tangible metric to track and evaluate over time. It can be used for both residential and commercial applications.

The formula is the following:

    Total Operating Expenses + Total Loan / Gross Scheduled Income (GSI)

Using some of the earlier numbers, the following can be calculated. Three units rent for GBS 1,000 (unit 1), GBS 900 (unit 2) and GBS 600 (unit 3), monthly. The asking price for the property is GBS 300,000.

| Years | 1 | 2 | 3 | 4 | 5 |
|---|---|---|---|---|---|
| Unit 1 | 12,000 | 12,000 | 12,500 | 12,500 | 12,500 |
| Unit 2 | 10,800 | 10,800 | 11,000 | 11,000 | 11,000 |
| Unit 3 | 7,200 | 7,200 | 7,400 | 7,400 | 7,400 |
| GSI | 30,000 | 30,000 | 30,900 | 30,900 | 30,900 |
| Vacancy 5% | 1,500 | 1,500 | 1,500 | 1,500 | 1,500 |
| Rental Income | 28,500 | 28,500 | 29,400 | 29,400 | 29,400 |
| Insurance | 800 | 800 | 800 | 800 | 800 |
| Management | 400 | 400 | 400 | 400 | 400 |
| Repairs 1% | 3,600 | 3,600 | 3,600 | 3,600 | 3,600 |
| Taxes | 0 | 0 | 0 | 0 | 0 |
| Agency Fees | 3,000 | 3,000 | 3,000 | 3,000 | 3,000 |
| Misc. | 500 | 500 | 500 | 500 | 500 |
| Total Expenses | 8,300 | 8,300 | 8,300 | 8,300 | 8,300 |
| NOI | 20,200 | 20,200 | 21,100 | 21,100 | 21,100 |
| Loan (mortgage) * | 15,024 | 15,024 | 15,024 | 15,024 | 15,024 |
| Cash Flow (before tax) | 5,176 | 5,176 | 6,076 | 6,076 | 6,076 |
| | 23,324 | 23,324 | 23,324 | 23,324 | 23,324 |
| Breakeven Ratio | 78% | 78% | 75% | 75% | 75% |

*Based on a 25-year mortgage of GBS 250,000 at an interest rate of 3.5%*

Figure 25. Example of the Breakeven Ratio

If we look at year one in the example above (Figure 25), our 78% ratio was calculated by adding the total annual operating expense of GBS 8,300 to the loan value of GBS 15,024. This amounts to GBS 23,324. This is then divided by the GSI of

GBS 30,000, thus giving us a breakeven occupancy ratio of 78%. This means that the combined properties could be up to 22% unoccupied, and you would still breakeven on costs. Exceed the 22%, and you would be losing money. In year three, the rent was increased, but the other costs stayed the same. This reduced the breakeven occupancy ratio to 75%. So now, you could have up to 25% of the properties unoccupied. The breakeven ratio can be applied to any potential investment proposition in any country providing you know the facts and figures.

## 63 Gross Rent Multiplier (GRM)

This is an easy calculation for a quick assessment of comparable properties. However, it doesn't account for cost factors such as maintenance, taxes, utilities and vacancy. It is essentially a ratio measurement between the property price and the gross scheduled income (GSI).

It is calculated as Property Price / GSI.

Let's use the figures from the table above.

Property price GBS 300,000 / GSI 30,000 (Combined monthly rent from each unit, 1,000 + 900 + 600 × 12 months).

So the GRM would be calculated as GBS 300,000 / 30,000 = 10.

This number, 10, indicates the number of years it would take for the rental income to equal the property price. The higher the number, the longer it will take. If the GSI were 20,000, it would take 15 years. For the purposes of evaluating several properties, you would be seeking the lowest GRM number.

As you can see, the GRM is quick and easy to calculate. However, because it is based upon the GSI only, it should merely be used as a guiding calculation. Remember, it ignores occupancy levels and operating expenses, both of which should be considered during any property investment analysis.

## 64 Buying Overseas

If you are tempted to buy overseas, using the calculations will go a long way in determining if the investment is a good one. However, you cannot always compare apples to apples. Buying in Dubai is not the same as buying in the UK or France or any other country for that matter. Each country has differing property laws, fees, regulations and taxes. Before any investment is made, you have to know what these are. Fortunately, or unfortunately, depending on the changes that occur, these can be beneficial or detrimental to your investment, both in the short and long term. Research all you can online about the country. If you make the decision to invest overseas, then seek legal advice prior to the purchase. Even then, be wary of investing in countries that experience political turmoil and civil unrest.

Even in stable countries with solid property laws, things don't always go to plan. The French rental market is a good example. It is extremely popular with the Brits and many other European neighbours. However, in recent years, it has seen a large increase in short- and long-term rental supply. A large portion of this has been fuelled by international owners who rent out their second homes. Inevitably, in some parts of the country (and on certain types of property), vacancy levels have increased, and investment returns have declined. This is certainly evident with short-term holiday lets, especially if they aren't in a prime location. So buying in a cheaper location may seem a good idea, but it's all about the numbers, and if they don't add up, you won't achieve a passive income. A good example would be investing in a ski resort. Property A is for sale at GBS 200,000 and is in a prime location, close to amenities and at the foot of the ski lifts. For argument's sake, property B is identical but 300 meters away. However, the price is GBS 180,000. It would seem like a good savings, but renting it out will always prove more challenging. People want convenience, especially on holiday. Three hundred meters is a long way to walk in ski boots, and savvy renters know it.

Buying an overseas property for personal use is obviously a wonderful opportunity. Those that do often seek to rent it out whenever it's vacant to cover the running costs and perhaps make a modest income. This is not an investment property, since it invariably gets used by the owner during the peak season, which diminishes returns. Vacancy rates are typically higher, so the chances are an overseas property used in this manner would barely break even. More likely, it would incur more expenditure than income. So always consider the property usage.

## 65 Holiday Lets

Holiday lettings remain very popular, especially in the south of France. These are referred to as a *location saisonnière*. Whilst you aren't required to supply a written tenancy agreement to holidaymakers, it is recommended. The law also states that the maximum duration of a holiday letting cannot be longer than three months. If it exceeds this period, it is considered to be the principal residence of the tenant and stricter regulations apply.

Unless you have an exceptional property with the 'charm' or 'wow' factor along with good management, then short-term lets can be risky. By risk, I am referring to long periods of vacancy, which we now know can have serious financial implications. After all, the strategy is for long-term passive income, not short-term gains.

Considerations must also be made for local property taxes in France. These are the *taxe d'habitation* and the *taxe foncière*.

The former is the residence tax, which is payable by the tenant; the property ownership tax, the *taxe foncière,* is paid by the landlord. If your property is empty, you may be liable for both. Even if you have a good grasp of the French language, completing and submitting the annual tax forms is no easy feat. I highly recommended using a qualified accountancy practice. These can be found online at: http://www.frenchtaxreturns.co.uk.

I haven't used the company personally, but they do offer a full range of accountancy, bookkeeping, business advice and tax advisory services. Instead, I use my father-in-law, a retired civil engineer and fellow landlord.

Whether buying in France or in any other country, the best type of property in which to invest is debatable. Rental properties, both old and new, can work; however, older properties often need the 'charm' factor to be rentable, whilst a modern new home is expected to offer the right amenities to a tenant, both within the property and the surrounding area.

Legal fees on new build property in France are currently low and amount, on average, to only 3.5% of the purchase price. This compares very competitively against 6% to 8% for an old property.

**Reasons to buy a new property:**

- 10-year building guarantee. New properties are built to comply with modern regulations, similar to the UK National House Builders Guarantee.
- It offers good insulation and uses low-maintenance materials, so the running costs are likely to be lower.
- Security—Gated complexes are quite common. They offer added protection to your property all year round.
- Often well-located—by the coast, next to a golf course or within a ski resort.
- Close to amenities.
- Easier property management, including guaranteed rental possibilities.

- Lower conveyancing fees—around 3% as opposed to 6–7% on older properties.
- Tax advantages under property management schemes.

**Reasons to buy an old property:**

- Character and setting of the property. Who doesn't want a French château surround by woodland and a nearby stream (or lake if you're really greedy)?
- There is the additional bonus of outbuildings and land.
- The price is often negotiable.
- Furniture may be included.
- Opportunity for renovation.
- The 'charm' factor.
- Ready to rent.
- No building wait period—unless it requires renovating.
- Traditional layout and sturdy build.
- Popular as holiday rental gîtes.

Whilst the French market is still a very attractive proposition, be aware that the total acquisition costs are usually around 7.0% higher than the listed price.

Let's consider an example:

One-bed apartment for EUR 120,000 (list price)

- Stamp duty 120,000 × 5.09% = EUR 6,108
- Notary's fees (120,000 × 0.83% + 411.35) × 19.65% VAT = EUR 1,683
- Notary's misc. = EUR 1,000
- Title deed (120,000 × 0.10%) = EUR 120

Therefore, the total acquisition cost (6,108 + 1,683+ 1,000 + 120) = EUR 8,911, which is 6.91% in addition to the list price. The total acquisition cost for the property would be EUR (120,000 + 8911) = 128,911.

When it comes to buying abroad, the bottom line is never buy with your heart—at least not when considering investment properties. Do your due diligence and consider the pros and cons before committing yourself.

Now, let's take this a step further and use some of the previous calculations to determine whether this one-bed apartment for EUR 120,000 is a good investment. Remember, for the most part, the calculations can be used in any country. Once you understand the cost structure, the rest should fall into place. For this example, I'll stay in France (the south) and work through the numbers. I have used EUR 845 for the monthly rental income. Here is my working spreadsheet (Figure 26), created in Microsoft Excel.

| Main Criteria | | | Annual Operational Costs | |
|---|---|---|---|---|
| Purchase Price | 120,000 | | Maintenance Fee | 150 |
| Down Payment % | 20% | | Management Fees | 0 |
| Down Payment | 24,000 | | Insurance Fees | 560 |
| Total Costs | 8,911 | | Repairs | 250 |
| Total Payments In | 32,911 | | Tax Fonciere - | 0 |
| Vacancy and Loss | 5.0% | | Tax d'habitation- | 680 |
| Annual Mortgage | 6,860 | | Misc Fees | 50 |
| Capital Expenditure | 0 | | **Total Op Expense** | 1,010 |

| Annual Income Description | Units | Rent (monthly) | Annual | % Rate of Occupancy | Total Ann Income |
|---|---|---|---|---|---|
| Unit 1 | 1 | 845 | 10,140 | 95.0% | **9,633** |
| Gross Scheduled Income (GSI) | | | 10,140 | Net Op Income (NOI) | 8,623 |
| Gross Operating Income (GOI) | | | 9,633 | Capitlisation Rate (CAP) | 7.19% |
| Gross Rent Mulitplier (GRM) | | | 11.83% | Cash Flow (before tax) | 1,763 |
| Break Even Ratio | | | 81.7% | Taxes (if applicable) | 680 |
| Cash on Cash | | | 5.4% | Cash Flow (after tax) | 1,083 |
| Gross Yield | | | 8.5% | Net Yield | 7.6% |

**Figure 26. Example Working Spreadsheet for a French Property Investment**

Let's break it down and take a look at the individual calculations.

## Main Criteria

- Purchase price: EUR 120,000—as advertised.
- 20% down payment—Based on an LTV of 80%. Calculated as EUR 24,000.
- Total cost: EUR 8,911—See total acquisition cost breakdown above.
- Total payments: EUR 32,911—Calculated as down payment + total costs.
- Vacancy: 5%—As per current market conditions.
- Annual mortgage: EUR 6,860—Refer to mortgage calculations section.
- Capital expenditure—Applied if renovations works are carried out.

## Annual Operational Costs

As outlined in the above spreadsheet, the annual operational costs include a maintenance fee (service fees) for the building's upkeep. They may also include management fees (if applicable), insurance, repairs, taxes and miscellaneous for the odd expenses. This information will vary from property to property, so the numbers should be as accurate as possible to properly evaluate the investment opportunity. The initial numbers can be obtained from various sources, including the real estate agent and the seller. Taxes have not been included in the costs.

**Annual Income**

- Gross scheduled income (GSI): 10,140—Calculated as the monthly rent 845 × 12 months. It doesn't include vacancy, so it's the maximum rent obtainable.
- Gross operating income: 9,633—Calculated as the percentage vacancy minus the GSI, so (10,140 − 507). Based on 5% vacancy.
- Gross rent multiplier: 11.83—Calculated as the property price 120,000 / GSI of 10,140. You would need comparable properties for this evaluation.
- Breakeven ratio: 81.7%—Calculated as (annual mortgage + total operating expenses) / gross operating income. Based on a 5% vacancy allowance, it means the property would need to remain 82% occupied. That's a total vacancy allowance of 18%.
- Cash on cash: 5.4%—Calculated as the cash flow before tax divided by the equity invested: 1,763 / 32,911 = 5.4%.
- Net operating income: 8,623—Calculated as the gross operating income minus the total operating expenses. See note below.

- Cap rate: 7.19%—Calculated as the net operating income divided by the purchase price. Refer to the section on Capitalisation Rate for more details.
- Cash flow (before tax): 1,763—your earnings calculated as your NOI minus your annual debt to service (mortgage). See note below.
- Taxes. It is essential to understand both the local and international tax implications for any investment property. By all means, do the research yourself, but ultimately seek legal advice. Taxes are complex, but in some cases, you may be entitled to a tax break without realising it.
- Cash flow (after taxes): 403—calculated as the cash flow (before tax) minus the taxes.

This leaves us with the gross yield and the net yield. It's surprising how many people get these two confused. More on them shortly.

## 66 Net Operating Income (NOI)

The mortgage loan, or debt to service, is not included in the NOI calculation. The NOI calculates the level of income the property would produce independent from any financing. This ensures that the income metric is the same for each property comparison. Therefore, the NOI is specific to the property and not to the buyer. Remember, the debt to service will be based on several factors, including the LTV, prevailing interest rate, loan period and loan type. This means it would be specific to the individual and not the property.

## 67 Cash Flow (before Tax)

The cash flow is the amount you would receive in profit (hopefully) at the end of the year. This is prior to any applicable taxes. The mortgage loan will affect cash flow based on the tenure period and interest rates, especially if these are variable rates. If you paid cash for the property and didn't take out a mortgage loan, then the cash flow would be equal to the NOI.

## 68 Cash-on-Cash

Cash-on-cash is another useful tool to learn, as you have seen demonstrated above. It is calculated by taking your cash flows and dividing them by the required cash equity amount needed to purchase the property. For many property investors, it is often the base calculation for their decision making. It's relatively quick and easy to perform and provides a means to compare the overall profitability of multiple investments.

Cash-on-cash can only be calculated properly once all the expenses have been determined. So, if you buy a new property, or one that needs negligible repair work, then you can run the numbers with a good degree of accuracy. However, if the property requires extensive repairs, then you may end up underestimating the final repair costs. Sometimes a seemingly simple repair can uncover a multitude of issues that then exceed the original budget.

It is important to remember that the cash-on-cash return is calculated by dividing the pre-tax cash flow by the amount of cash invested (or down payment plus costs) and that it is expressed as a percentage. The cash-on-cash return calculation is as follows:

Pre-tax cash flow / total cash invested = cash-on-cash return

For example, in the above table, which is based on a property of EUR 120,000, I have the following breakdown:

- Deposit (down payment)   24,000
- Costs                    8,911

Total Costs: 24,000 + 8,911 = 32,911

- Calculated cash before tax  1,763

If I invested EUR 32,911 into a new property and earned EUR 1,763 per year in cash flow before taxes, then that's a 5.4% cash-on-cash return (1,763 / 32,911). Cash-on-cash simply looks at the cash return from the property and compares it to the cash invested. It's one of several important return ratios that measure investment opportunities, so you should practise using it.

Let's look at another example comparing a cash purchase to a mortgaged one.

Property A: Purchased with Cash (GBS 110,000)
Price: GBS 100,000
Costs: GBS 5,000
Repairs: GBS 5,000
Total Cash Invested: (100,000 + 5,000 + 5,000) = 110,000

*Pre-Tax Cash Flow Calculation:*
Gross scheduled income (GSI) = 13,200 (based on a monthly rent of 1,100)
Less: physical vacancy/other losses (5% of GSI) = 660
= effective gross income of 12,540 (13,200 – 660)
Plus: other income 0 (if applicable)
= gross operating income of 12, 540
Less: operating expenses of 900 (insurance etc.)
= net operating income of 11,640
Less: annual debt service of 0 (mortgage free)
= pre-tax cash flow of 6,640.

*Cash-on-Cash Return Calculation:*

Pre-tax cash flow / total cash invested = cash-on-cash return

GBS 6,640 / GBS 110,000 = 6% cash-on-cash return

Property B: Purchased with a Mortgage (LTV 80%)

Price: GBS 100,000

Costs: GBS 5,000

Repairs: GBS 5,000

Total Cash Invested: (20,000 deposit + 5,000 + 5,000) = 30,000

*Pre-Tax Cash Flow Calculation:*

Gross scheduled income (GSI) = 13,200 (based on a monthly rent of 1,100)

Less: physical vacancy/other losses (5% of GSI) = 660

= effective gross income of 12,540 (13,200 – 660)

Plus: other income 0 (if applicable)

= gross operating income of 12, 540

Less: operating expenses of 900 (insurance)

= net operating income of 11,640

Less: annual debt service of 5,817 (based on a 80,000 loan at 4% interest for 30 years)

= pre-tax cash flow of 2,057.

*Cash-on-Cash Return Calculation:*

Pre-tax cash flow / total cash invested = cash-on-cash return

GBS 2,057 / GBS 30,000 = 8.2% cash-on-cash return

In summary:

Property A—Cash purchase 110,000 with a pre-tax cash flow of GBS 6,640, resulting in a 6% cash-on-cash return.

Property B—Mortgaged for 80,000 with a pre-tax cash flow of GBS 2,057, resulting in an 8.2% cash-on-cash return.

Therefore, as I have illustrated above, by using financing there is a trade-off between the monthly cash flow and the cash-on-cash return.

I consider the cash flow analysis a key tool. It should be used to ensure a healthy bottom line before making an investment. The steps are reasonably straightforward. You will require the NOI and your annual debt to service (mortgage) rate. Once the cash flow (before tax) is calculated, you will have a realistic outlook on the investment opportunity. The resulting number should be used in conjunction with the other calculations we have covered. The steps:

Step 1

Calculate the monthly mortgage rate of the property.

Step 2

Calculate the annual gross scheduled income (GSI).

Step 3

Calculate the annual gross operating income (GOI). This is the GSI minus the percentage vacancy.

Step 4

Calculate the total operating expenses (TOE).

Step 5

Calculate the net operating income (NOI). This is the GOI minus TOE.

Step 6

Calculate your annual debt to service (mortgage).

Step 7

Subtract the debt to service from the annual NOI to give you the cash (before tax).

## 69 Gross and Net Yields

The gross yield expressed as a percentage is unquestionably the simplest calculation to perform. It is achieved by dividing the annual rent by the property price. Let's say we found a property for GBS 120,000 that commanded a monthly rent of GBS 185.

The annual rent would be 185 × 52 (weeks) = GBS 9,620.

The gross yield would be 9,620 / 120,000 = 0.080, or 8.0%.

I have seen many targeted advertisements for investment properties aimed directly at potential investors that often highlight the rental yield. Sometimes the ads will claim: 'Earn a 24% yield in only three years', but the 8% yield in the above example for one year seems worthwhile. However, some unscrupulous individuals will use gross rental yields to deliberately entice potential investors, especially vulnerable novices.

Remember this is 'gross yield'; it doesn't take into account any costs associated with the property—this makes it seem enticing.

We have seen from past examples that costs are an integral part of the picture. Consequently, it is the net yield that you should focus on. The biggest of these costs is likely to be the mortgage, followed by ongoing costs such as maintenance, insurance, service charges, agency fees and so on. Let's say our total operating expenses (TOE) are GBS 4,600. If we factor these into the equation, we can calculate the net yield.

(GSI) 9,620 – (TOE) 4,600 = GBS 5,020

So the net yield would be: GBS 5,020 / GBS 120,000 = 0.041, or 4.1%.

In my opinion, this is not a particularly attractive net yield. In some cases, the figure could also turn out negative. This could happen, for example, if you took out a mortgage for only 15 years instead 25 years, or as a result of higher-than-anticipated costs. The lower the mortgage term, the higher the monthly payment. This, in turn, results in a lower net rental yield.

We have looked at a few examples, and I am sure that you have realised that I haven't painted the brightest picture in terms of property investment. That's simply because I wanted to keep it balanced. Providing examples with exceptional returns gives false hope. Everyone's definition of 'exceptional' will vary. The point I am trying to make is that finding the right investment property is possible almost anywhere. To do so, you should understand the investment criteria. The good news is that deals are always out there, and you should now have the fundamental skills needed to find them.

At this point, you may be asking: 'What constitutes a good ROI?' The answer depends on your goals. Let's say you placed GBS 20,000 into a savings account at your bank. I doubt you would earn more than 4% interest, and that's being generous. I don't know anyone personally that has retired happy and content by doing this. Similarly, you could invest that same amount into the stock market or any other interest-bearing scheme. The returns, as you know, would vary and are almost impossible to predict. However, with any property we can calculate our returns. You have greater control over the investment and ultimately its ROI.

The use of spreadsheets for doing calculations has become ubiquitous. It's a simple way to get quick results. Use any of the major search engines, and you'll invariably find a free online calculator for what you are seeking. Mortgage payments are a typical example. Plug in some numbers, like loan value and term length, and the calculation is done instantly, thereby revealing a plethora of information. However, understanding those numbers is imperative if you really want to build your property portfolio.

Find an online calculator, or build your own. Start plugging in some realistic numbers, then vary the mortgage amount, term length and interest rate. You'll soon see the outcome variances and, hopefully, learn how they would affect you. As an exercise, gather as much information as you can on a few properties and run the numbers. You should be doing this before seeking to buy your first property. If you are planning on buying in the area in which you live, then it should be simple to source the necessary information from either your local estate agents, local newspaper or a good website portal.

However, if you are familiar with Microsoft Excel, then building your own spreadsheet to calculate the generated returns is easier than it may seem. You can even break it down into segments, as I have done below. The example provided is for a Dubai-based investment and allows for input changes based on current and future regulations and their associated costs. The transfer fee, as administered by the Dubai Land Department (DLD), used to be 2% but was increased to 4% in 2013, whilst the mortgage arrangement fee has remained at 0.25% of the loan value. However, you can adapt the spreadsheet to suit your own market.

To generate some realistic results, I have used some current valuation figures and my Dubai calculator.

Unlike most other countries, Dubai, or rather the UAE, does not have 'taxes' on property—yet. However, there are transaction fees and other fees associated with buying and selling property. What are the current fees associated with buying a property in Dubai and how do they impact our investment decision? Let's take a look.

Target Property—One-bedroom
- Price: GBS 1,250,000
- Rental value: GBS 100,000

### Property Calculator - Part 1

| | | |
|---|---|---|
| Valuation Fee | 3,000 | Enter Value |
| Transfer Fee (DLD)* | 4.00% | % of the Purchase Price |
| Mortage Arrangement Fee | 0.25% | % of the Loan |
| Enter the Property Cost | 1,250,000 | Enter Value |
| Agency Fees (*often 2%*) | 1% | Enter % Value |
| Transfer Fee | 50,000 | (Cell E10 x E6) |
| Mortgage Fee | 2,344 | (Mortgage Loan Value x E8) |
| Valuation Fee | 3,000 | (Value of cell E4) |
| Agent Fees | 12,500 | (Cell E12 x E10) |
| Other Fees | 0 | |
| | | Notes |
| Total Costs | 67,844 | (Sum of cells D14:D18) |
| Total Property Cost | 1,317,844 | (Sum of cell E10 + E20) |
| Costs as a Percentage | 5.15% | (Cell E20 /E22) |

\* (DLD) - *Dubai Land Department.*

**Figure 27. Example Dubai Property Calculator—Part 1**

## Property Calculator - Part 2

### Main Criteria

| | |
|---|---|
| Purchase Price | 1,250,000 |
| Down Payment % | 25% |
| Down Payment | 312,500 |
| Total Costs | 67,844 |
| Total Payments In | 380,344 |
| Vacancy and Loss | 3.0% |
| Annual Mortgage | 65,188 |
| Capital Expenditure | 0 |

** Part 3

\* Refer to Part 3

### Annual Operational Costs

| | |
|---|---|
| Maintenance Fee | 14,000 |
| Management Fees | 0 |
| Insurance Fees | 7,500 |
| Repairs | 3,000 |
| Misc fees | 1,500 |

- Leave at 5% if your unsure

| | |
|---|---|
| Total Op Expense | 26,000 |

### Annual Income

| Description | Units | Rent (monthly) | Annual | % Rate of Occupancy | Total Ann Income |
|---|---|---|---|---|---|
| Units | 1 | 8,333 | 100,000 | 97.0% | 97,000 |
| Gross Potential Income | | | 100,000 | Net Operating Income | 71,000 |
| Gross Operating Income | | | 97,000 | Capilisation Rate (CAP) | 5.68% |
| Gross Rent Mulitplier (GRM) | | | 12.50% | Cash Flow (before tax) | 5,812 |
| Break Even Ratio | | | 94.0% | Taxes (if applicable) | 0 |
| Cash on Cash | | | 1.5% | Cash Flow (after tax) | 5,812 |
| **Gross Yield** | | | **8.0%** | **Net Yield** | **5.9%** |

**Figure 28. Example Dubai Property Calculator—Part 2**

The purchase price and the associated costs from Part 1 (Figure 27) are then transposed to Part 2 (Figure 28), leaving only a few highlighted cells to be completed. Once this is done, these should reveal the primary calculations required for your assessment. The mortgage (debt to service) is calculated separately in Part 3 (Figure 29), and elements are also transposed to Part 2.

## Property Calculator - Part 3

### Repayment Mortgage
Calculate the loan information assuming a constant yearly rate

| | | |
|---|---|---|
| Mortgage Loan Value | 937,500 | |
| Interest Rate | 3.49% | Enter Value |
| Years ( max 20 years ) | 20 | Enter Value |
| Payments per Year | 12 | Enter Value |
| Total Payments | 240 | (Cell AB12 x AB14) |
| Monthly Payments * | 5,432 | See PMT formula above |
| Total Payments Value | 1,303,753 | (Cell AB18 x AB16) |
| Cost of Mortgage | 366,253 | (Cell AB20 - AB8) |

**Figure 29. Example Dubai Property Calculator—Part 3**

The main page tells me that to buy this property I would need approximately GBS 380,000 in available cash, which is a combination of GBS 312,000 for the down payment plus GBS 68,000 in costs. So, if I had GBS only 320,000 available, I would need to look elsewhere.

It is worth adjusting the numbers to see the impact of certain differences—for example, if you could secure the mortgage for 30 years instead of 25 or if you could secure a lower interest rate than the 3.45% mentioned. Savings made through negotiation do have a profound impact, especially in the longer term. This makes them worth exploring.

## 70 Net Present Value

Let's throw one more equation into the mix. This is called NPV, which stands for net present value. It requires its own workings and is slightly more complex to understand. NPV is often used by investors wishing to calculate an investment return on a risk-adjusted basis. In other words, a discounted rate is applied to each period of investment (usually years), which converts the future value (FV) back to the present value (PV). This allows you to evaluate an investment with a predetermined and desired rate of return. It is expressed as a value and not as a percentage. It will also provide one of the following outcomes:

1. A value greater than zero—This means that the discounted value of the future cash flows is greater than the initial investment. In other words, you're getting a higher rate of return than anticipated. Pursue this opportunity.

2. A value equal to zero—This means that the discounted value of the future cash flows is exactly equal to your initial investment. In other words, you're getting your exact return. This investment would be worth further review.

3. A value less than zero—This means that the discounted value of the future cash flows is less than the initial investment. In other words, the return is less than you desired. This investment is not worth pursuing. Walk away.

To determine the NPV, let's look at the calculation and the different methods we can use to obtain it:

PV (present value) = discounted factor × FV (future value)

Let's put it into practice.

We have property for GBS 80,000 with estimated cash flows for each of the following five years. Our desired return is 6% on this investment.

We have three basic methods to calculate the NPV. The first is to use a discount table as shown below (Figure 30). These can easily be found online. Find the corresponding discount rate for each period required. In the example table, I have used the 6% over a five-year period. Our first-year discount rate would be 0.943, as shown.

| Periods | 5% | 6% | 7% | 8% | 9% | 10% |
|---|---|---|---|---|---|---|
| 1 | 0.9524 | 0.9434 | 0.9346 | 0.9259 | 0.9174 | 0.9091 |
| 2 | 1.8594 | 1.8334 | 1.8080 | 1.7833 | 1.7591 | 1.7355 |
| 3 | 2.7232 | 2.6730 | 2.6243 | 2.5771 | 2.5313 | 2.4869 |
| 4 | 3.5460 | 3.4651 | 3.3872 | 3.3121 | 3.2397 | 3.1699 |
| 5 | 4.3295 | 4.2124 | 4.1002 | 3.9927 | 3.8897 | 3.7908 |
| 6 | 5.0757 | 4.9173 | 4.7665 | 4.6229 | 4.4859 | 4.3553 |
| 7 | 5.7864 | 5.5824 | 5.3893 | 5.2064 | 5.0330 | 4.8684 |
| 8 | 6.4632 | 6.2098 | 5.9713 | 5.7466 | 5.5348 | 5.3349 |

Figure 30. Example (NPV) Discount Rate Table

Create a simple spreadsheet (Figure 31) and fill in the corresponding rates. The -80,000 represents our initial outflow of cash for the investment at period zero (present).

The cash inflow for the first year is 21,000. After applying the discount rate from the above table, the present value would be 19,811 in year 1. The process is repeated for each year.

| | | | |
|---|---|---|---|
| | **Net Present Value - Discount Rate** | | |
| Desired return as a percentage | | 6% | |
| Period Years (t) | Future Value (FV) | Discount Rate | Present Value (PV) |
| 0 | -80,000 | | |
| 1 | 21,000 | 0.9434 | 19,811 |
| 2 | 19,000 | 0.8901 | 16,912 |
| 3 | 22,000 | 0.8396 | 18,471 |
| 4 | 15,000 | 0.7921 | 11,882 |
| 5 | 22,000 | 0.7472 | 16,438 |
| **Outflows** | -80,000 | **Inflows** | 83,514 |
| So our resulting NPV would be the Outflow + Inflow = | | | 3,514 |

If NPV > 0      Then accept
If NPV < 0      Then reject

The result of 3,514 means our return is higher than the 6% originally desired.
Note: Rounding off the discount rate will impact the resulting NVP calculation.

Figure 31. Example NVP Calculated Rate using the Discount Table

I have used only a short five-year example. In most cases, the period would be 10 years or more. It is also important to note that the FV cash value can also be a negative number.

The second method (Figure 32) of calculating NPV is to use a direct formula. Instead of using the discount rate from the tables, we would instead apply a formula to achieve the discount rate. Again, this can be done in Microsoft Excel.

First, take your desired % return (in our example 6%) and convert this to a decimal. So 6/100 = 0.06 (r)

Use the formula PV = FV/([1+r]t) to calculate the PV.

| Period Years (t) | Future Value (FV) | PV=FV/((1+r)t) | Present Value (PV) |
|---|---|---|---|
| | | Net Present Value - Discount Rate | |
| Desired return as a percentage | | 6% | |
| 0 | -80,000 | | |
| 1 | 21,000 | 19811.321 | 19,811 |
| 2 | 19,000 | 16909.932 | 16,910 |
| 3 | 22,000 | 18471.624 | 18,472 |
| 4 | 15,000 | 11881.405 | 11,881 |
| 5 | 22,000 | 16439.680 | 16,440 |
| Outflows | -80,000 | Inflows | 83,514 |
| The resulting NPV would be the Outflow + Inflow = | | | 3,514 |

The PV for year 1 would be 21000/((1.06)^1) = 19,811
The PV for year 2 would be 19000/((1.06)^2) = 16,910
The PV for year 3 would be 22000/((1.06)^3) = 18,472
The PV for year 4 would be 15000/((1.06)^4) = 11,881
The PV for year 5 would be 22000/((1.06)^5) = 16,440

See applied calculation formula for cells D8 - D12

Note: Rounding off the discount rate will impact the resulting NVP calculation.

Figure 32. Example of NVP using the Formula Method

As expected, the results are the same as when using the discount table method.

Our final method (Figure 33) is to use the formulas within Microsoft Excel. If you have tried the above methods, they should help with your understanding of how the NPV is calculated. We can use Microsoft Excel to calculate our NPV given that cash flows are evenly spaced over time. Using the same outflows and inflows as above, the example provided below shows how easy it is to calculate NPV in Excel. Note the NPV formula in cell D12.

### Example of Net Present Value

| Years | Cash Flow | | |
|---|---|---|---|
| 0 | -80,000 | Outflow | |
| 1 | 21,000 | Inflow * | Note: * An inflow can also be a negative number. |
| 2 | 19,000 | Inflow | |
| 3 | 22,000 | Inflow | |
| 4 | 15,000 | Inflow | |
| 5 | 22,000 | Inflow | a) If the value of NPV is greater than 0, then the project is profitable and worth the risk. |
| 6 | 0 | Sale Value | |
| Discount Rate | 6% | | b) If the value of NPV is less than 0, then the project isn't worth the risk. |
| NPV | 3,513.96 | | |

Remember NPV is a way to decide whether or not to invest in a project by looking at the projected cash inflows and outflows.

**Figure 33. NVP Calculation**

So what does NPV really tell us? It simply helps us to decide whether or not a new project is financially viable. The NPV measures the potential gain or loss that a property investment could produce. The results are often compared to what could be earned by keeping the money in a bank or another investment opportunity that generates a return equal to the discount rate.

Interpreting the results of the calculations can only come from practice, but the real bonus is that they work internationally. Wherever you plan to invest, you now have another evaluation tool to add to your arsenal.

I have given examples using French property; however, other European countries, like Portugal and Spain, also offer some very good investment opportunities at present. I am not personally familiar with the Portuguese market, but I know through friends that sites like http://meravista.com provide plenty of information to any would-be investor. Many would argue that now is a good time to invest in Greece. With the Greek financial system in turmoil, many savvy investors are snapping up choice properties—especially beachside ones—and for relatively little money in comparison to other popular Mediterranean countries. Remember the chapter on the property cycle? Well these investors are counting on the Greek economy recovering, in which case property prices will surely rise. It is a buyers' market, I wouldn't dispute that, but then again I don't know the market. So on a personal level, for me the risk is too high. Buying a property because it seems like a 'bargain' will, more often than not, come back to haunt you. Basic online research is fine, but back this up with personal advice.

## 71  Making an Offer

Once you have found the right property, the next step is to make an offer. How you draft the offer letter will really depend on where in the world you live. The 'letter of intent', 'offer letter' or whatever other terminology is used to describe it, is geared toward the goal of securing the property for purchase. In some countries, a verbal agreement and handshake may be the only thing required; but sadly, in the ever-growing world of legalities, it is prudent to be prepared. In some countries, the offer letter may be legally binding, so it is often drafted by a solicitor or lawyer; in other countries it's not even a requirement. Regardless, the intent of the letter is generally the same and often includes the following information:

- The legal address and a description of the property
- Details regarding the offer price and terms

- A mandate that the seller will provide clear title to the property
- Details regarding costs or other fees between the buyer and the seller
- The date and time the offer will expire
- Any contingencies that the deal is subject to

The last point is very important. I believe there are three main insertions that should always be added.

1. At the offer stage, you should also ask them to take the property off the market. They don't have to agree to this, but doing so will debar other potential buyers.
2. The second is to include the provision that the sale is contingent on you qualifying for a loan. Even if you have conditional approval from the bank, it will bring peace of mind if your personal circumstances should suddenly change.
3. Finally, you should include that the sales agreement is subject to all due diligence being completed satisfactorily.

Once you have submitted the offer and assuming the negotiations are proving positive, the seller will want to see progress. For this reason, try to avoid any unnecessary delays in getting the surveys and other legal work completed.

## 72 What Happens after Finding a Property?

There are always good deals to be found, so have patience—your deal will inevitably come along. Prior to starting your search, you should already have a clear plan of what you are looking for and how it will be financed. Once you have found a suitable property, it's paramount that you conduct a complete and accurate due diligence on it. If you are unfamiliar with the market or residential investment properties, then this is a good time to engage a professional agency.

Here is a list of some of the considerations:

- **Rental Income Analysis**

If the property has been rented before and you have the income and expenses statements, you can ascertain quite quickly whether the property is worth pursuing further.

- **Inspection**

Do a thorough site walk and compile a damage report. You can do an initial visual inspection yourself, noting any minor or major damage.

- **Property Valuation**

Even if your inspection didn't reveal any major concerns, if you are still considering buying the property, then you should proceed with a full structural survey and valuation. Appointing an independent and certified valuation expert to assess the value of a property can help you negotiate the best price, reduce risk and save money.

- **Capital Renovations**

Based on the inspection and valuation report, determine how the requirement for additional capital will affect your bottom line. Also, consider if any work undertaken will add value.

1. Conduct a Title Search.

    Don't assume that everything is included in the sale. Make sure you that identify what's for sale—including parking spaces and storage facilities—and ensure that this is reflected in the title search.

2. Market Analysis.

    Understand what is happening in the local market. A market that is saturated with investors, for example, will reduce your chances of having a successful rental.

It is easy to become caught up in the emotion of buying a property. Sometimes in the eagerness to move forward, shortcuts are made—often unknowingly.

If I were buying a property in Paris, for example, it is easy to go online to find the pricing information for a specific area, street and even building (Figure 34). Whilst this is only a guide, it is very useful to spot potential areas that are becoming popular and hence likely to increase in value. As you can see from the map below, the lowest cost area (marked in green) is worth EUR 6,085 per m² compared to EUR 13,454 per m² (marked in red) nearer the heart of Paris.

**Figure 34. Illustration of Area-Specific Pricing**

If I were buying in Dubai, then websites like http://www.justrentals.com/, https://www.propertyfinder.ae/ and https://www.bayut.com/ provide excellent listings and valuable pricing information covering most areas and buildings.

I am sure that this is also the case in many other countries. However, regardless of which country you invest in, one of the most important aspects of the due diligence process is checking the numbers.

## 73 Buying an Existing and Tenanted Investment Property

If you are planning to buy a rental property that is already tenanted, then it should be easy to get a hold of the income and expenditure statements.

Let's say I had GBS 12,500 ready as a deposit. The seller asks for GBS 60,883 for the property. They also provide the following information:

    Total operating expenses: GBS 1,750

    Annual income: GBS 5,400

If we run the numbers, we should get the following:

**Sellers Offer**

| | | |
|---|---|---|
| Purchase Price | 60,883 | Enter price |
| Down Payment % | 20.00% | Enter % of downpayment |
| Down Payment | 12,177 | |
| Other Costs | 0 | Enter any other costs |
| Total Payments In | 60,883 | |
| Vacancy and Loss | 0% | Enter % value (5% if unknown) |
| **Total Op Expense** | 1,750 | Information from seller |
| Monthly Loan Payments (Mortgage) | 257 | Calculated from mortgage table |
| Annual Loan Payments | 3,085 | Calculated cell E18 x 12 (months) |
| **Monthly Income** | 450 | Information from seller |
| **Annual Income** | 5400 | Calculated cell E22 x 12 (months) |
| Gross Potential Income | 5400 | Cell E24 |
| (Vacancy amount) | 0 | Cell E14 |
| Gross Operating Income | 5400 | Calculated cell E26 -E28 |
| (Other Income) | 0 | If known |
| NOI | 3650 | Sum of cell (E30 +E32)-E16 |
| CAP Rate | 6.00% | If known or calculated |
| Property Value | 60,833 | Cell E34 / E36 |
| (NOI - Annual Loan) | 565 | Cell E34 - E20 |
| Cash on Cash | 4.64% | Cell E40 /E8 |

Figure 35. Example Calculation of Cash-on-Cash using Seller's Information

The table in Figure 35 shows a positive income. In fear of being gazumped, some people would panic and buy the property immediately. A few months down the line, it would become evident that the property is not living up to their expectations. As it transpires, the property had not been properly maintained, and the operating expenses originally provided were found to be underestimated. The rental income provided was the gross potential income, which is the potential income if the property is let 100%. In the real world, this is never the case. Consequently, no allowance for vacancy was allocated. If we adjust the numbers to take these into consideration, we can compare them to the revised cash flow (before tax). As you can see from Figure 36 below, it's not looking very promising.

|  | Seller | Actuals | |
|---|---|---|---|
| Purchase Price | 60,883 | 60,883 | |
| Down Payment % | 20.00% | 20.00% | |
| Down Payment | 12,177 | 12,177 | |
| Other Costs | 0 | 0 | |
| Total Payments In | 60,883 | 60,883 | Applied % vacancy for the area |
| Vacancy and Loss | 0% | 8% | |
| **Total Op Expense** | 1,750 | 1850 | Adjusted operating expenses |
| Monthly Loan Payments (Mortgage) | 257 | 257 | |
| Annual Loan Payments | 3,085 | 3,085 | |
| **Monthly Income** | 450 | 450 | |
| **Annual Income** | 5400 | 5400 | |
| Gross Potential Income | 5400 | 5400 | Calculated as cell (G26 x G14) |
| (Vacancy Amount) | 0 | 432 | |
| Gross Operating Income | 5400 | 4968 | GOI now adjusted for vacancy |
| (Other Income) | 0 | 0 | |
| NOI | 3650 | 3118 | NOI also gets adjusted |
| CAP Rate | 6.00% | 6.00% | Based on actual operating expenses and allowing for vacancy, the offer prices should have been in the region of GBS 52,000 |
| Property Value | 60,833 | 51967 | |
| (NOI - Annual Loan) | 565 | 33 | |
| Cash on Cash | **4.64%** | **0.27%** | |

Figure 36. Example Calculation of Cash-on-Cash Using Adjusted Information

Using the cap rate, which is typical in the US approach, the purchase price should have been around the GBS 52,000 mark. Therefore, accepting income and expense statements from a seller or agent without verifying them first can be costly. However, I'm an optimist, so let's think on the positive side.

Let's say we did our due diligence and, having adjusted the numbers, we conveyed our findings in a polite manner to the seller. He agrees to sell for GBS 52,000, and we use the same down payment of 12,177. Now, let's take a look at the revised numbers.

|  | Seller | Actuals | Offer | |
|---|---|---|---|---|
| Purchase Price | 60,883 | 60,883 | 52,000 | Revised offer to seller |
| Down Payment % | 20.00% | 20.00% | 20.00% | |
| Down Payment | 12,177 | 12,177 | 12,177 | Note: Required downpayment would be less at GBS 10,400. However for the example I have used the same GBS 12,177 |
| Other Costs | 0 | 0 | 0 | |
| Total Payments In | 60,883 | 60,883 | 52,000 | |
| Vacancy and Loss | 0% | 8% | 8% | |
| **Total Op Expense** | 1,750 | 1,850 | 1,850 | |
| Monthly Loan Payments (Mortgage) | 257 | 257 | 210 | |
| Annual Loan Payments | 3,085 | 3,085 | 2,520 | Adjusted mortgage rate |
| **Monthly Income** | 450 | 450 | 450 | |
| **Annual Income** | 5400 | 5400 | 5400 | |
| Gross Potential Income | 5400 | 5400 | 5400 | |
| (Vacancy Amount) | 0 | 432 | 432 | |
| Gross Operating Income | 5400 | 4968 | 4968 | |
| (Other Income) | 0 | 0 | 0 | |
| NOI | 3650 | 3118 | 3118 | |
| CAP Rate | 6.00% | 6.00% | 6.00% | |
| Property Value | 60,833 | 51,967 | 51,967 | The Cash-on-Cash is now looking more positive. |
| (NOI - Annual Loan) | 565 | 33 | 598 | |
| Cash on Cash | **4.64%** | **0.27%** | **4.91%** | |

**Figure 37. Example Calculation of Cash-on-Cash with Revised Offer Price**

Now our cash flow has increased considerably, and the cash-on-cash is looking healthier (Figure 37). To free up even more cash, you could opt for an interest-only mortgage, as shown in cell K18, below (Figure 38). This would have an even greater impact on cash flow and the cash-on-cash return.

|  | Seller | Actuals | Offer | Interest |
|---|---|---|---|---|
| Purchase Price | 60,883 | 60,883 | 52,000 | 52,000 |
| Down Payment % | 20% | 20% | 20% | 20% |
| Down Payment | 12,177 | 12,177 | 12,177 | 12,177 |
| Other Costs | 0 | 0 | 0 | 0 |
| Total Payments In | 60,883 | 60,883 | 52,000 | 52,000 |
| Vacancy and Loss | 0% | 8% | 8% | 8% |
| **Total Op Expense** | **1,750** | **1,850** | **1,850** | **1,850** |
| Monthly Loan Payments (Mortgage) | 257 | 257 | 210 | 133 |
| Annual Loan Payments | 3,085 | 3,085 | 2,520 | 1,596 |
| **Monthly Income** | **450** | **450** | **450** | **450** |
| **Annual Income** | 5400 | 5400 | 5400 | 5400 |
| Gross Potential Income. | 5400 | 5400 | 5400 | 5400 |
| (Vacancy Amount) | 0 | 432 | 432 | 432 |
| Gross Operating Income | 5400 | 4968 | 4968 | 4968 |
| (Other Income) | 0 | 0 | 0 | 0 |
| NOI | 3650 | 3118 | 3118 | 3118 |
| CAP Rate | 6% | 6% | 6% | 6% |
| Property Value | 60,833 | 51,967 | 51,967 | 51,967 |
| (NOI - Annual Loan) | 565 | 33 | 598 | 1522 |
| Cash on Cash | **4.64%** | **0.27%** | **4.91%** | **12.50%** |

**Figure 38. Example Calculation of Cash-on-Cash with Interest-Only Mortgage**

Maintaining the property going forward could mean a reduction in operating expenses or at least keeping them constant. A well-maintained property can often command a higher rent, so in practice, the cash flow on this property could increase further.

## 74 The Purchase

I remember the boom days in Dubai leading up to the financial crisis of 2009. This period underscored property as one of the most sought-after asset classes in the city. People would carry a chequebook to any and all new property launches in the hope of scoring a bargain. It seemed like everyone wanted a slice of the pie, and the developers knew it. It got to the point that people would buy literally anything to get on the property ladder. It was purely speculative investing, and it seemed like the majority of speculators had no idea what they were doing. Many bought off-plan property without even seeing it. Let me illustrate the point. Imagine 10 small apartment blocks in a row, each 50 meters apart. All apartments are priced equally. You have run your numbers, and the ROI looks good. The first block has exceptional views of a golf course and lakes. The second building has partial views of both. The third only has a partial view of the golf course, and the fourth has no view at all. By the time you reach the tenth building, the views are of an adjacent sewage works. If you had the choice, which building would you choose? I think the answer is fairly obvious, but let's assume building 1 had already sold out. Would you buy into building 2? Sometimes the buying frenzy can be such that people are willing to buy anything, even if it's in building 10.

So how could our fictitious developer and agent sell apartments in building 10, especially those that are next to the sewage works? Unbeknownst to many, it often just comes down to the use of clever words in the advertisement. Consider the following:

- Building 10 with lake facing apartments.
  Or,
- Building 10 with lake views.

The sellers would use 'lake facing', not 'lake views', to describe the building. Technically, it's facing a lake, so that can't be disputed. The fact that nine other buildings are blocking the view is irrelevant. So the next time you see apartments with sea 'facing' views as opposed to a sea 'views', now you'll know the difference.

The point in making this analogy is simple. Sometimes you just have to walk away. Sadly, I have heard of many people simply buying in the hopes of selling shortly thereafter and making a profit. In other words, speculating. Sometimes it works; sometimes it doesn't. Who would want to be left holding a property facing a sewage works, knowing that they paid the same price as someone in building 1 who has a golf course and lake view? I can almost guarantee that anyone buying in building 10 didn't do their due diligence, and I would bet my bottom GBS that they don't understand investment basics, such as gross potential income, gross operating income, net operating income, cap rate, cash flow, cash-on-cash, gross yield, net yield and, of course, NPV. That is why I'm now confident that I won't find you buying property in building 10.

## 75 Motivated Sellers

Unless I am buying a new property, I will always seek motivated sellers. In essence, a motivated seller is a person that has a strong desire to sell their property, often quickly. There are many reasons explaining why someone would want to sell quickly, but truthfully, it is rather rare that a seller's motivation will dramatically affect the price of a property. That said, it comes down to individual circumstances. More often than not, it's due to time constraints. Here are some reasons that a seller may be motivated:

- The seller is moving (job relocation, overseas posting, or military assignment).
- The seller is going through a divorce or having relationship problems.
- The property is nearing foreclosure.
- The seller is facing bankruptcy.
- The seller has bought another property and doesn't want two mortgages.
- The seller inherited the property and is looking for a quick sale.
- There has been a death in the family.
- The seller has an illness.
- The seller has lost his job.
- The seller needs cash (for a multitude of reasons).

Understanding why the seller is motivated is paramount. If it's a time constraint situation, such as relocation, bankruptcy or foreclosure, then you may be able to use this information to craft a win-win offer on the property. Playing hardball with low offers will almost always fail. It's all about establishing a degree of trust with the seller. For example, if I knew that they had to relocate within a month, I would make my offer stating that I would have everything completed within 30 days or less.

This time period should resonate with their needs and appear to relieve some of the burden from their shoulders. If it does, your work is almost done. If it's a good deal for both of you, then settle on the terms and move forward as agreed. Don't make false promises, especially if you know you can't honestly fulfil them.

## 76 Ripple Effect

When seeking investment properties, consider the 'ripple effect'. Imagine a pond as a city or town with the most expensive properties right in the middle. When people can no longer afford to live in the more expensive centre, they move outward. In this case, to the surrounding suburbs. As they buy into the cheaper neighbouring suburb, prices begin to increase, and the process is repeated in adjacent suburbs—just as the ripples of a pebble dropped in the centre of a pond expand outward. Anticipating these growth areas can be very lucrative, but it's all about timing.

We have covered enough now to understand the fundamentals. The next step is understanding how to build the portfolio.

## 77 Setting your Goals

There comes a point when you have done the reading, played with the numbers and you are finally ready to start. The key here is to be realistic. Building your property portfolio takes time. So set one goal at a time. Having realistic goals at this stage is essential. That is why I have deliberately kept this book balanced, or at least tried to. Some will heed my advice; others won't. Perhaps I should have emphasised the word 'realistic' when describing the importance of having realistic goals. Unless you have experienced a large windfall, trying to accelerate the process by buying several properties in the first year is not going to work. Instead, aim for one really good property in your first year. This will be your foundation property. If you are in your later years and have some disposable income, then being a little more aggressive in your purchases (providing you've done the math) won't hurt. Whether you buy a couple of investment properties or several hundred in your lifetime, I can guarantee one thing: you will always remember the first one. Setting a goal will also keep you focused. It should also provide the incentive to save to make the all-important payments. Your plan will be dictated by many factors, including demographics, salary, family commitments and your own desire. That's why there are no hard and fast rules. As time moves forward, the plan can change, but don't lose focus.

## 78 Losing Focus

In 2005, due to some unforeseen circumstances, I thought I was going to lose my job. I was earning a good income from my properties and had a sizable sum ready to invest further. I don't know whether it was the indecisiveness of the day or the new business opportunity that loomed, but I ended up investing in a business I knew nothing about. The business was advanced automated DVD rentals. The machines looked like ATMs, only sleeker in design—just as you would expect from an Italian company. The price tag matched the looks. I went into the venture with two other partners, and we secured the rights for the Middle East region. We had done the sums, and the bank said the business plan was one of the best they had ever seen. I thought we had factored in everything, and I was feeling very confident. Dubai was going through a boom and times were good, but the reality soon became clear. The prime locations we had planned to set up our machines were owned by two large companies. The annual rent they wanted for the 1 m² space that the machine would occupy equated to 5,000 DVD rentals. Yes, 5,000 DVD rentals just to break even. The very source of rental income I aspired to was now taunting me. Needless to say, with the advent of on-demand movies and the number of pirated downloads taking place at the time, the business ended up being liquidated after a couple of years. I lost a sizable sum of money, but ultimately, I had lost focus.

I have learned my lesson. There is no point in looking back and having regrets, but I do know that I did miss some very good property investment opportunities.

## 79 Setting Up as a Company

The size of your property portfolio obviously lies with you. As I have stated previously, it could be anything from one property to several hundred. It could be a very modest property next door or several investment properties scattered overseas. Either way, the aim should be to optimise any tax liabilities, present and future. One way to do this is to form a company and have the properties bought and registered under the company name. This would make sense if you were looking to grow your portfolio, as it would be more tax efficient to hold the properties under a company name.

The question remains as to whether you should group your properties under a Limited Liability Company (LLC).

Unfortunately, it's not easy to move existing properties into a company. In the UK, capital gains would apply, which could make the exercise prohibitively expensive.

In Dubai, they would need to be mortgage free and registered under an offshore company account. In France, you would need to declare the tax regime under which the rental properties would fall. Each country will have different laws, so it is worth seeking some professional advice from the outset.

**The Advantages**

- The main advantage of an LLC, as seen by many, is asset protection. Having protection is important, especially in the US where tenants are more prone to litigation, but there are alternatives.
- Tax advantages. This will depend on where the property is and under which jurisdiction it falls.
- LLC's are easier to form and keep in good legal standing.
- One of the long-term advantages of buying rental properties under an established company is that you can make your children or grandchildren shareholders.

**The Disadvantages**

- The cost structure for setting up an LLC will inevitably vary from country to country. There may also be restrictions on jurisdiction.
- You may not be able to transfer existing property assets without incurring further costs. This is especially true of properties that are already mortgaged.
- Your access to lenders and the mortgage options may be restricted, as the lending risk will be further evaluated.
- An LLC may not protect you from potential lawsuits.

Whether you decide to go down the company route or operate as an individual, you will need one essential element for protection: insurance.

## 80 Insurance

Whilst I may only understand the basic workings of insurance, I do recognise its importance. I also know that it is often overlooked by property investors and landlords, even though it should be a vital part of building your successful property portfolio. In the unlikely event of a property loss, whether it's partial or total, if you are not properly insured you could find yourself financially distressed—and in some cases, that's putting it mildly.

If you don't take out insurance, then think about how you would manage financially if you were faced with hundreds or even thousands of Globals in damage to your rental property or if you became unable to re-let your property while extensive repairs were being made.

On a global level, insurance policies will vary, but some exclusions, limits and conditions will apply, so you will need to choose a policy that best meets your needs. Buying a property in a known flood area is an obvious example of where you would take out flood insurance. Here are some other elements to consider:

- Storms
- Lightning
- Fire
- Earthquake
- Explosion
- Impact
- Escape of liquid or dangerous chemicals
- Malicious acts, riot, and civil commotion
- Legal liability

The reason that some people don't take out insurance is that they assume it will be very expensive. But property insurance isn't as expensive as you may believe. Tailoring the policy to your needs can further reduce costs, rather than taking out an all-inclusive policy. Additional properties can often be added to a single main policy, thereby further reducing costs. In general, the more properties you insure, the lower the premium.

A good landlord insurance policy should include the following:

- **Public liability insurance**
  This provides cover should a tenant, visitor or worker become injured or their belongings be damaged as a result of a fault in your property.
- **Loss of rent cover**
  This provides cover should your property become uninhabitable due to damage, for example, fire or flood.
- **Contents insurance**
  This is recommended if you provide furnished accommodation. It should cover the contents as well as fixtures and fittings. Otherwise, tenants should have their own contents insurance for items they keep on the property.

Suffice it to say, it's a bit like finding a good broker. Making sure you've got the right level of cover is paramount; the last thing you need is to worry about is whether your policy will pay out—especially if the worst has already happened. Don't automatically assume you'll be covered, and, if in doubt, it's better to be over-insured than underinsured. Shop around and ask questions before signing on the dotted line. Of course, you won't need insurance until you have found the right property to purchase.

## 81 Finding the Right Properties

If you recall, I made a statement at the beginning of the book arguing that a passion for property could be a good thing or bad thing. So what is the bad part of this passion? Before I give my answer, let me ask one more question. Have you ever visited an old or run-down property that is for sale? If so, what went through your mind as you made your visit? If you're like me, as you walked through the door you could begin to visualise its potential. It would seem, however, that most people don't have this ability. Instead, almost the opposite is true—they can't see its potential, and they certainly can't visualise what could be achieved by buying it. I remember buying one such property in France many years ago. It was very run-down with a poor layout. It required a complete renovation throughout. Of course, my friends were curious to see what I had bought and soon came visiting. As I gave them the tour, I explained the detailed changes I was planning to undertake. At this stage, everything was in my head, including a costing estimate. But all I could see was the horror on their faces. They really couldn't visualise the house. The interesting part, however, was that when the property was completed, sure enough, my friends revisited the house. This time, not only did they compliment me on the finish, but they recalled just how I had said it would look. In fact, I had made very few changes to the original ideas. Nowadays, I don't buy properties that need renovating. I find it too time-consuming and labour intensive. However, I still see huge potential in many properties that I visit. That's the bad thing about being passionate for property investing. If you are looking for a property that requires renovation, it's often far too easy to get caught up in the emotion behind the purchase. It has to be about the numbers. Remember, this is a business, and property is your trade. On the flip side, if you really can't see the potential in an old run-down property, then that's a good thing, because you will only base your buying decisions on the numbers. If you really want to buy property for renovation, be sure to have someone to consult that can point out the potential—but not the current owner!

## 82 Buying and Renovating

If your preference is the renovation of older properties for rental, then do so. Be warned, however. If this is your first venture into the world of renovation, make sure you have a structural survey done. Carrying out a personal inspection with some 'expert' friends may reveal nothing. In reality, the property could appear to be in very good condition. At this stage, emotions often surface that subconsciously drive the deal forward. All the while, hidden from view could be some serious problems, including the following:

- **Subsidence**

Older homes can be prone to a variety of foundation and structural problems, such as major cracks or unevenness in the slab or perimeter foundation wall.

- **Dry rot**

Homes exposed to excessive moisture especially over prolonged periods often develop mould and mildew.

- **Plumbing**

The older the home, the greater the likelihood of finding a substandard plumbing system; the mains feed may even feature lead pipes.

- **Electrical**

Older homes can have outdated junction boxes and switches and sometimes inadequate grounding. They are also more susceptible to the wiring insulation deteriorating over time. This poses both a safety risk and leads to a having a substandard electrical system.

- **Roof damage**

This is often hard to see without direct roof access. Problems stemming from a compromised roof, particularly once interior leaks begin, include pest infestations, interior water damage and compromised insulation.

- **Single-pane windows**

These offer poor insulation and ultimately make for a cold house. The simple solution is to replace the old windows with more efficient double-glazed ones, but these can be expensive.

Combine all the above problems that are typically associated with an older property and you can appreciate that renovation costs would soon add up. These potential problems, however, could all be detected by having a survey done. It could save you from some real financial exposure. Yes, it will cost to have the survey done, but if problems are detected, you can use this to your advantage when negotiating the final purchase price—assuming you still want to buy it.

The rewards of renovating an older property can be very personally and financially gratifying. However, depending on the degree of renovation required, it can also be very time-consuming. Don't forget to factor in the lost rental income during the period of renovation.

If you are looking for a renovation property, then definitely look for one with hidden potential. This could be a loft conversion or a building extension, for example. Any costs must be offset by the ability to apply a rent increase and ultimately achieve regular passive income.

I had one such space a few years ago in France. It was a loft space in the building I owned. It had a floor-to-ceiling height of 6 meters (nearly 20 ft.). The roof was pitched with exposed wooden trusses. It was completely open plan, which meant having free reign at the design stage. After a couple of weeks of sketching out options, I settled on a layout that incorporated a mezzanine level for the bedroom and storage area. To optimise the space, I also wanted to install a spiral staircase.

With a clear layout defined, I sought three quotes for the work. It required dry lining, complete electrics, plumbing, tiling, bathroom fitting, kitchen unit installation and, of course, the spiral staircase. From experience, I already had a good idea of what the total cost should be. Although I would always recommend three, get at least two quotes and make sure they are from reputable companies.

When I got the quotes back, they were fairly close and certainly in line with what I had anticipated. What separated them was the completion time. One company quoted over six months, another four months and the final company three months. I had the work completed in exactly three months and a couple of weeks later it was rented to one very happy tenant. Prior to conversion, the property value was around EUR 75,000. The conversion cost was just under EUR 50,000, and it rented for EUR 618 per month. The cash-on-cash return came in at 12.9%, and three years later, the market value of the property was EUR 118,000. Some projects are clearly worth doing.

Assuming you still want to go down the path of renovating, then you should follow these basic guidelines:

- Use professional tradesmen if you don't have the necessary time and skills.
- Get three quotes for the work.
- Seek properties with extra hidden potential.
- The finished interior decorating should be done in neutral colours.
- The kitchen and bathroom form the core of the house and should be done to a good standard.

- Relocate bathrooms in older properties to suit modern day needs.
- Use modern energy efficient lighting.
- Use mirrors to create the illusion of space.
- Consider parking needs.
- Don't forget the math—is it viable?

## 83 Property Secrets

If you are reading this then I envisage that one of two scenarios has taken place. The first is that you have diligently read from the start of the book and have just reached this chapter. Congratulations! The second is that you have opened this book, browsed through the contents and having seen the chapter on 'Property Secrets', thought you would have a sneak preview in the hopes of unlocking the path to property wealth. Well, I am sorry to disappoint you. If there are any secrets, please share them with me. Rather than use the word 'secret', perhaps 'strategy' would be better. However, what I can say is that anyone can make modest or serious money from property if they follow a few key strategies and stay focussed. Those strategies are covered within this book.

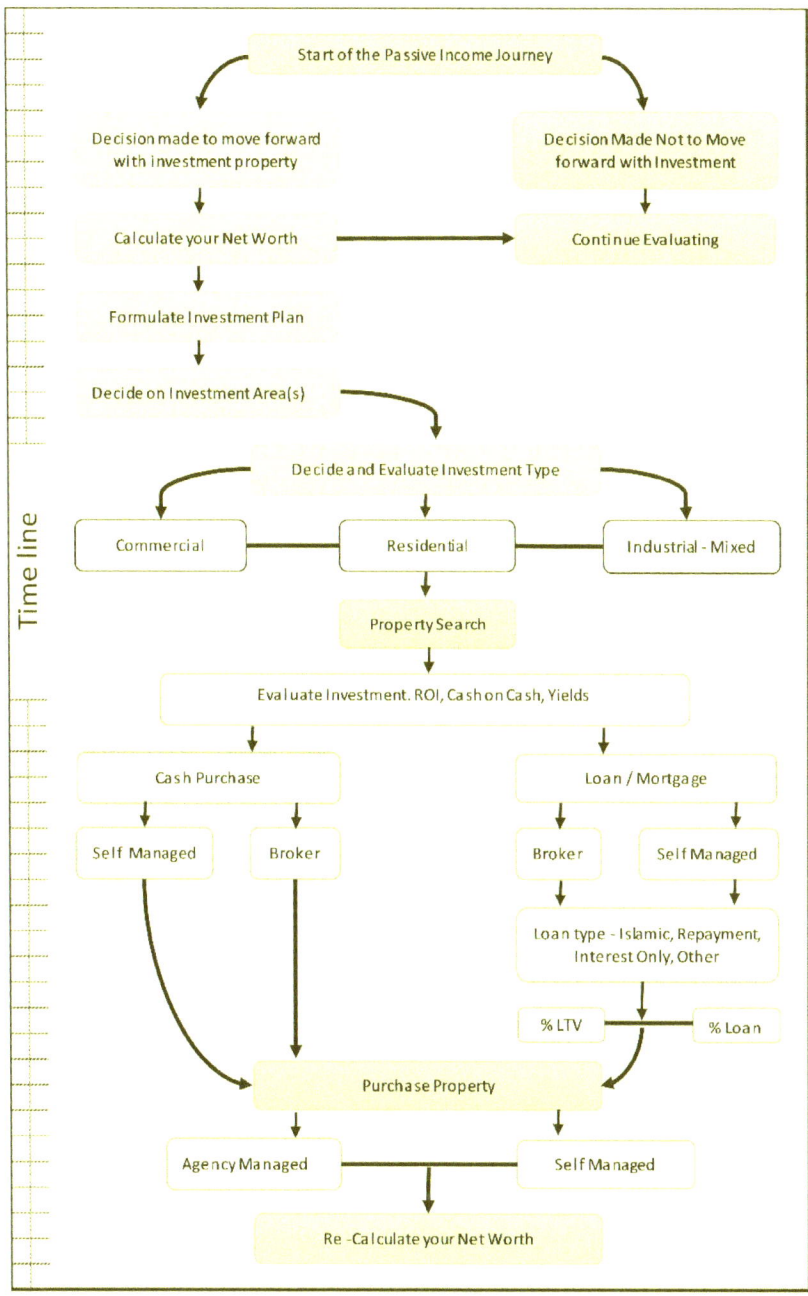

**Figure 39. The Journey Flow Chart**

## 84 The Property Business Question

Near the beginning of this book, I asked what you thought would happen if I gifted USD 60,000 to 10 random strangers and asked them to buy the best ROI investment property they could find for the money. Compare your answer now. Is it still the same?

First, let's take a step back and ask if these are the only options. I didn't say you couldn't add any additional funds. If you had an LTV of 80%, then you could finance a property worth up to USD 250,000. Another option would be to divide the USD 60,000 and put deposits of USD 30,000 down on two investment properties. The possibilities go on.

What really matters, however, is the investment potential and that comes down to the numbers. In this case, the numbers are the cash flow, with the cash flow simply being the income and expenses. If you don't analyse these investment numbers prior to making a purchase, then you could end up with a negatively geared investment.

## 85 Frank and Betty: The Investors

Let's assume for the following scenario that we are going to buy residential property. Our young property investor at the age of 25 is called Frank, and he's been putting aside GBS

10,000 per year for the last three years. He now has GBS 30,000 in savings to use as a deposit. Frank's partner, whom he has just married, is called Betty. She is also 25 and about to start work. From next year, she will manage to save GBS 7,500 per annum. They are currently renting a modest two-bed property.

If we assume that the bank offers them an LTV of 75%, then they could potentially buy a property costing up to GBS 120,000. However, as we've learned, it's not about buying the most expensive property, it's about considering our return on investment. Moreover, it's about whether the property will generate the passive income required.

After doing some research, they find the following property:

Property **A** details—One-bed apartment in immaculate condition and vacant.
- Asking price: GBS 65,000
- Buying costs are 4.5% of the purchase price (generic example)
- Down payment: 25%
- Vacancy and voids in the area are at 5%
- Insurance quoted at GBS 480

- Annual repair fund contingency at GBS 600, miscellaneous costs at GBS 50
- Rental income per month is GBS 480
- Mortgage term: 25 years
- Interest rate: 3.6% (repayment mortgage from Bank X)
- Annual taxes are equivalent to one month's rent (generic example)

The cap rate in the area is 5.98%. So would this be a good investment for Frank and Betty? Can you work out the following?

1. Does it follow the 1% rule?
2. What is the total property cost?
3. What is the down payment, including costs?
4. How much is their annual mortgage?
5. What are their total operating expenses?
6. What is the cap rate?
7. What is our cash flow (before tax)?
8. What is the gross yield?
9. What is the net yield?

1. Let's start with the 1% rule. **1% Rule = monthly rent / cost of the property**

480 / 65,000 = 0.74%. So no, it does not pass the 1% rule.

2. The total property cost = **the buying costs + purchase price**

The buying costs are 4.5% of the 65,000 purchase price = 2,925

2,925 + 65,000 = 67,925 (see Figure 40 below)

3. The down payment and costs = **25% of the purchase price + costs**

25% of 65,000 = 16,250. Add the costs of 2,925 = 19,175

4. The annual mortgage would be 2,960 (using MS Excel PMT function)
5. The total operating expenses = **insurance + repairs + miscellaneous**

480 + 600 + 50 = 1,130

6. The cap rate = **net operating income / purchase price** (expressed as a percentage)

4,342 / 65,000 = 0.0668 or 6.8%

7. To determine cash flow before tax, you would first need to work out the following:

**(NOI − annual loan) − capital expenditure (CE)**

(4,342 − 2,960) − CE (as we have don't have any CE, the result would be 1,382)

8. Gross yield = **annual rental income (monthly income × 12) / property value × 100**

5,760 / 65,000 × 100 = 8.86%

9. Net yield = **(annual rental income − annual expenses) / (total property costs) × 100**

(5,760 − 1,130) / 65,000 × 100 = 7.12%

Overall, their potential investment looks good.

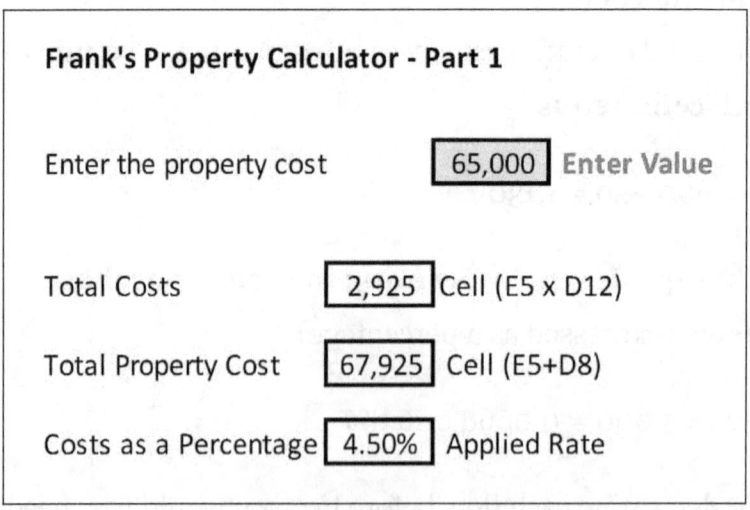

Figure 40. Frank's Property Calculator − Part 1

They have a positive cash flow of GBS 1,382 before tax (Figure 41).

### Frank's Property Calculator - Part 2

| Main Criteria | | | | Annual Operational Costs | |
|---|---|---|---|---|---|
| Purchase Price | 65,000 | | | Maintenance Fee | 0 |
| Down Payment % | 25% | | | Management Fees | 0 |
| Down Payment | 16,250 | | | Insurance Fees | 480 |
| Total Costs | 2,925 | *Part1 | | Repairs | 600 |
| Total Payments In | 19,175 | | | Misc Fees | 50 |
| Vacancy and Loss | 5.0% | | | Total Op Expense | 1,130 |
| Annual Mortgage | 2,960 | ** Part 3 | | Capital Expenditure | 0 |

| Annual Income Description | Units | Rent (monthly) | Annual | % Rate of Occupancy | Total Ann Income |
|---|---|---|---|---|---|
| Unit 1 | 1 | 480 | 5,760 | 95.0% | 5,472 |
| Gross Potential Incom (GPI) | | | 5,760 | Net Operating Income | 4,342 |
| Gross Operating Income | | | 5,472 | Capilisation Rate (CAP) | 6.68% |
| Gross Rent Mulitplier (GRM) | | | 11.28% | Cash Flow (before tax) | 1,382 |
| Breakeven Ratio | | | 74.7% | Taxes (if applicable) | 480 |
| Return on Equity Invested | | | 4.7% | Cash Flow (after tax) | 902 |
| Gross Yield | | | 8.86% | Net Yield | 7.12% |

**Figure 41. Frank's Property Calculator – Part 2**

## Scenario 1.

- The old tenant leaves after five years, and the rent is increased to GBS 510, as per the market rate, for the new tenant.

| Annual Income Description | Units | Rent (monthly) | Annual | % Rate of Occupancy | | Total Ann Income |
|---|---|---|---|---|---|---|
| Unit 1 | 1 | 510 | 6,120 | 95.0% | | 5,814 |
| Gross Potential Incom **(GPI)** | | | 6,120 | Net Operating Income | | 4,684 |
| Gross Operating Income | | | 5,814 | Capilisation Rate (CAP) | | 7.21% |
| Gross Rent Mulitplier (GRM) | | | 10.62% | Cash Flow (before tax) | | 1,724 |
| Breakeven Ratio | | | 70.3% | Taxes (if applicable) | | 510 |
| Return on Equity Invested | | | 6.3% | Cash Flow (after tax) | | 1,214 |
| Gross Yield | | | 9.42% | Net Yield | 5.00% | 7.68% |

Figure 42. Frank's Property Calculator – Revised Rent

Now we have increased cash flow (Figure 42). Our breakeven ratio has reduced, meaning the property can be vacant longer yet the income will still cover the outgoing costs. The yields have also increased along with our return on equity invested.

## Scenario 2.

In addition to the rent increase, Frank and Betty took out an interest-only mortgage instead of the repayment mortgage.

Frank's Property Calculator - Part 3

| | Repayment | | Interest Only |
|---|---|---|---|
| Mortgage Loan value | 48,750 | | 48,750 |
| Rate | 3.60% | | 3.60% |
| Years ( max 20 years ) | 25 | | 25 |
| Payments per year | 12 | | 12 |
| Total Payments (months) | 300 | | 300 |
| Monthly Payments | **247** | or | **146** |
| Total Payments | 74,003 | | |
| Cost of Mortgage | 25,253 | | |

Figure 43. Frank's Property Calculator – Interest Only Mortgage

With a repayment mortgage, their monthly payments are GBS 247, equating to an annual payment of GBS 2,964. If they had taken out an interest-only mortgage, then their monthly payments would be considerably lower, at GBS 146 (Figure 43), which equates to GBS 1,752 per annum. This has bolstered their bottom line; however, it comes with risk. Remember, they still need to pay back the capital at the end of the mortgage period. As a result, investors taking out an interest-only mortgage often rely on capital appreciation to bridge the gap. They do this when market conditions are deemed favourable.

To illustrate this point, look at the table from Nationwide below. You can clearly see the house price trend for the UK. If Frank and Betty had bought a house in February 2005 with an interest-only mortgage, then by 2015 they would have gained around 40,000 in capital appreciation. However, if they had bought in mid-2007, then by mid-2014 they would have little, if any, capital appreciation.

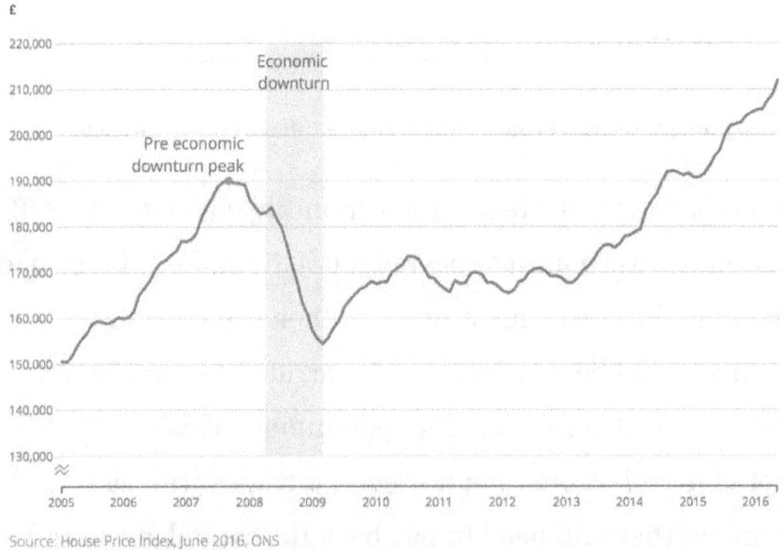

Figure 44. Office for National Statistics Average UK house prices

By taking out an interest-only mortgage, they would have GBS 2,929 in cash flow before tax (Figure 45). Some investors use this strategy to build cash flow; in turn, this is used towards the down payment on additional properties.

| Annual Income Description | Units | Rent (monthly) | Annual | % Rate of Occupancy | Total Ann Income |
|---|---|---|---|---|---|
| Unit 1 | 1 | 510 | 6,120 | 95.0% | **5,814** |
| Gross Potential Incom (GPI) | | | 6,120 | Net Operating Income | 4,684 |
| Gross Operating Income | | | 5,814 | Capilisation Rate (CAP) | 7.21% |
| Gross Rent Mulitplier (GRM) | | | 10.62% | Cash Flow (before tax) | 2,929 |
| Breakeven Ratio | | | 49.6% | Taxes (if applicable) | 510 |
| Return on Equity Invested | | | 12.6% | Cash Flow (after tax) | 2,419 |
| Gross Yield | | | 9.42% | Net Yield | 7.68% |

**Figure 45. Frank's Property Calculator – Increased Cash Flow**

As you can see, the type of mortgage taken out can have a big impact on cash flow.

If Frank had saved the money for an outright purchase, it would have taken him six and a half years without any contribution from Betty. That's assuming house prices remained stable.

If we apply what we have learned so far, then it should be apparent that the fundamentals are the same, but each journey is different. I guess that's what I like about this medium- to long-term strategy. It's not defined; you buy what you can afford and when you can afford it.

## 86 Building the Passive Income

By now, I am sure that you have a reasonable understanding of what we have already covered. You can also appreciate that there are many paths that one can take, but for now, I will go down only one. It's about managing risk. I will put forward a simple case study using my fictitious couple, Frank and Betty. This will be done over a 10-year period. Moreover, as we lead them down the road of passive income; you can decide the level of risk that they should take.

**Year One**

Let's assume Frank and Betty bought property **A** (a one-bedroom apartment) when market conditions were favourable. They paid GBS 65,000. They took out a repayment mortgage at 3.6% for 25 years. They rented the property for GBS 510 per month.

Frank has been putting aside GBS 10,000 per year for the last three years. His partner Betty will save GBS 7,500 per annum from year two.

**Year Two**

In year two, Frank and Betty didn't buy property but continued to save.

**Year Three**

Frank and Betty are now 27 years old. Over the last couple of years, they have gained a considerable understanding of their local property market. They are ready to invest further. A local builder is completing a new development in the heart of the city. On offer are some well-appointed apartments. The one-bedroom apartments are selling for GBS 80,000. Frank and Betty make a direct offer with the developer to purchase the show apartment. It means a delay of four months before they can take possession, but they agree on a sale price of GBS 76,000. It's also a win for the developer, who gets cash flow prior to completion of the whole complex and gives him a sale on his books.

Property **B** details—One-bed apartment.

- Asking price: GBS 80,000 (negotiated to 76,000)

- Buying costs are 4.5% of the purchase price (generic example)
- Down payment: 25%
- Vacancy and voids in the area are at 5%
- Insurance quoted at GBS 500 + misc. expenses at 600
- Rental income per month is GBS 520
- Mortgage term: 25 years (repayment)
- Interest rate: 3.65% (repayment mortgage from Bank X)

One factor to consider is how much they had saved prior to buying this property. Property A required a down payment of 25%, which came to GBS 16,250. The buying costs came to GBS 2,925, which added up to a total of GBS 19,175. If you recall, they had saved GBS 30,000, so they still had GBS 10,825 in savings left over.

In addition, Frank continued to save GBS 10,000 and Betty GBS 7,500 per annum. Therefore, their total savings, not considering their income prior to purchasing property B, was GBS 45,825. After deducting the total payment for property B, at GBS 22,420, they are still left with GBS 23,405. That's why, in the following year, they buy a studio in the same complex for GBS 58,000.

**Year Four**

Property **C** details—Studio apartment.

- Asking price: GBS 60,000 (negotiated to 58,000)
- Buying costs are 4.5% of the purchase price (generic example)
- Down payment: 40% (they elect to make a high down payment)
- Vacancy and voids in the area are at 5%
- Insurance quoted at GBS 460
- Rental income per month is GBS 430
- Mortgage term: 20 years (repayment)
- Interest rate 3.30% (lower repayment mortgage due to higher deposit)
- Annual taxes are equivalent to one month's rent

**Years Five and Six**

In years five and six, Frank and Betty continue to save. They have started a family, and so their combined savings have dropped from GBS 17,500 per annum to GBS 7,500.

They also spend GBS 1,000 for repairs to property A from year 5 onward. At the end of year six, without tax adjustments on earnings taken into consideration, they still have approximately GBS 46,000 in savings.

**Year Seven**

Property **D** details—One-bed apartment.

- Asking price: GBS 90,000 (paid 88,000)
- Buying costs are 4.5% of the purchase price (estimated)
- Down payment: 25%
- Vacancy and voids in the area are at 5%
- Insurance quoted at GBS 600 + misc. expenses at 600
- Rental income per month is GBS 540
- Mortgage term: 20 years (repayment)
- Interest rate: 3.50% (repayment mortgage from Bank Y)

**Years Eight, Nine and Ten**

Frank and Betty don't buy any more property, but they continue to manage their existing portfolio of properties. They now own three one-bedroom apartments and one studio. They manage the properties themselves.

Here's the summary:

| | |
|---|---:|
| Properties owned | 4 |
| Total value (assumes 4% appreciation) | 374,947 |
| Outstanding property loans | 135,675 |
| Equity | 239,272 |
| Cash flow (before tax) | 6,492 |
| Cumulative cash flow (savings plus rental income) | 82,278 |

They are now both 35 years old, and they have a healthy balance sheet. At this stage, they could do one of the following:

- They could stick to the same formula for the next 10 years.
- They could consider releasing their current equity to make even more aggressive purchases.
- They could refinance their existing properties if rates are favourable.
- They could start paying off the mortgages quicker to be debt free sooner.
- They could just sit back and manage the properties as they are, whilst slowly paying off the mortgages.
- They could stop renting and buy their own property.

As I have maintained from the beginning, the answer to this question is a personal choice and one that should be undertaken after considering the risks, both long- and short-term. So, do you think they took big risks? Do you think they are in a more secure financial situation than a comparable couple that hasn't saved or invested in property?

I know some people will say that it's probably not practical to save GBS 10,000 per year, as illustrated. True, for some it's not; but had Frank and Betty saved even half this amount, then buying studios instead of one-beds would have certainly been both feasible and a good option. The other important consideration is the yield. In the graph below (Figure 46), I have plotted 15 random properties in the south of France. It shows that studios generally have a better overall rental yield than one-, two- or three-bed apartments.

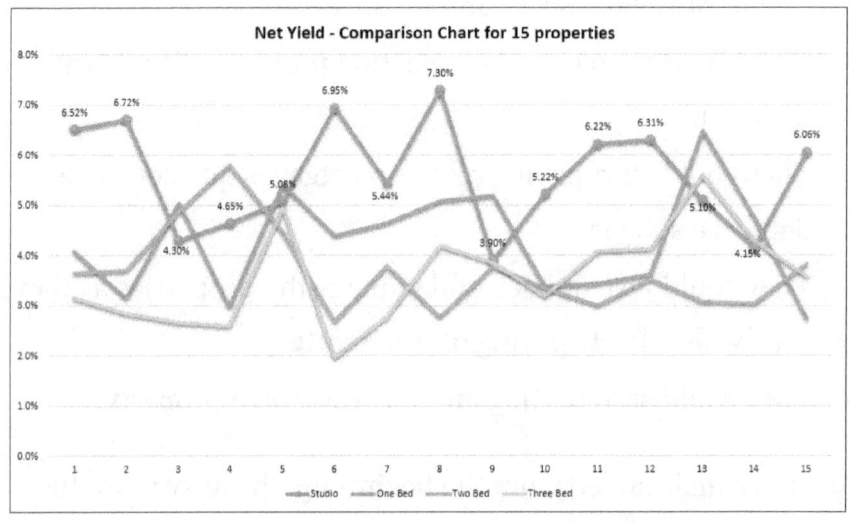

Figure 46. Example Comparison of 15 Random Properties Showing Rental Yields

## 87 Start by Renting, not Buying

Let's stick with Frank and Betty a little longer and consider one further aspect of their situation: their own housing needs. Most young people aspire to owning their own home. This is certainly true in the UK, which is a country as seemingly obsessed with property as France is obsessed with food. However, getting a foot on the property ladder is no easy feat in many countries. Consequently, building a property portfolio would seem to be an impossible dream for many, especially for those in their early twenties. Nevertheless, aspirations of owning a home seem to remain. The result is that many young people end up stretching themselves beyond their means just to acquire property. Ultimately, they end up struggling to maintain their payments in the hope that property prices will rise so they can re-mortgage. The real question is, are there any other options?

It may seem counterintuitive, but renting a property can be beneficial in the early and later stages of investing. If Frank and Betty had decided to buy their own property first, then the money saved, in this case GBS 30,000, would have been used to pay the deposit, costs and annual mortgage payment in year one. This would be followed by subsequent mortgage payments. The result is that it would have deferred their ability to buy any passive income properties for a few years, at least.

Now, at 35 years old, they can either continue renting or use the equity and savings they have built up to buy their own home.

Let's jump forward another decade. Frank and Betty have been actively buying property and have a sizeable portfolio of

20 properties. They have GBS 500,000 in equity and cash flow. They have always wanted an ocean view villa in the south of France. The villa in question costs GBS 1,600,000. Assuming they proceed with the purchase, they would be looking at the following costs:

Purchase price: GBS 1,600,000 (for scenario 1 GBS = 1 Euro)

Down payment at 25% = GBS 400,000

Costs (approximately): GBS 70,000

Annual mortgage: 84,256 (based on a repayment mortgage of 20 years at 3.6%)

Monthly mortgage payments would be GBS 7,021

Rental Income: 0

Yes, they would have a lovely home and hopefully an appreciating asset. But let's suppose they rent out the property instead. If you recall, I stated that the rental income from different sized properties is not linear. In other words, if a 20 $m^2$ studio rents for GBS 350 per month (350/20 = GBS 17.5 per $m^2$), then a large villa of 250 $m^2$ should rent for GBS 4,375 per month (250 × 17.5 per $m^2$). The reality is far from it. The villa would probably rent for less than half that amount. For argument's sake, let's say it rents for GBS 2,150 per month, or GBS 25,800 per annum. Now it becomes affordable for tenants.

There comes a time when you need to enjoy the fruits of your labour. Assuming they could buy the villa for GBS 1,600,000, they would have a substantial asset—one that would hopefully continue to appreciate over the years. They could even hand it down to their children. But, they would be paying a large mortgage for another 20 years. The costs associated with buying the property would eat heavily into their equity and cash flow. On the other hand, if they rented out this fabulous property for GBS 25,800 per annum, they would still have the equity and cash flow to buy other investment properties, if they so desired. This would leave enough money to do the things in life they enjoy.

If I were Frank and Betty, I would be renting the fabulous property in the south of France and enjoying life. So what's next?

## 88 Invest Further or Pay Down Loans?

This question can easily divide a room. Like much of what we have already discussed, it comes down to personal preference. The factors that enter the equation include level of risk, interest rates, property cycle, asset valuation, your retirement goals and cash flow, to name a few. Whether you reinvest in more property or pay down your existing assets, it should be a win-win, because you will ultimately be reinvesting in yourself.

Let's use our wonderful couple, Frank and Betty, to help illustrate the point. After 10 years, they have met their goals and have four mortgaged properties. At this stage, many investors lose their focus and discipline. Some will use the passive income to buy liabilities rather than assets, like a new car or a bigger TV. That's fine—you have earned it—but these investors will often find that within a very short period of time their expenditure starts to break even, or even exceed their income. In this situation, should interest rates suddenly rise, they could find themselves owing more than they actually earn, especially if they have taken on additional loans. It could put their assets at risk. It's probably not a surprise to learn that many people are often left with no choice but to keep paying down their mortgages beyond their original terms.

As we know, Frank and Betty are far more disciplined. They have at least another 10 years before the first mortgage is paid down, but they decide to speed up paying down the first mortgage by increasing their monthly payment. Let's recap.

In year one, they paid GBS 65,000 for the property.
Then, they took out a repayment mortgage of GBS 48,750 at 3.6% for 25 years.

They rented the property for GBS 510 per month.

The total mortgage payments would be GBS 74,003, and the mortgage cost would be GBS 25,253.

If they increased their monthly payments after 10 years from GBS 247 to GBS 347 (an increase of only GBS 100 per month), then the total payments would be reduced to GBS 70,312 and the mortgage cost reduced to GBS 21,562, representing a savings of GBS 3,690. However, the real savings is time. The remaining 15 years would be reduced to 9.8 years. In other words, they would be mortgage free 5.2 years sooner.

On the other hand, if they increased their monthly payments even further after 10 years from GBS 247 to GBS 547 (an increase of GBS 300 per month), then the total payments would be reduced to GBS 67,622 and the mortgage cost reduced to GBS 18,872. This would give them a savings of GBS 6,381.This time, the remaining 15 years would be reduced to 5.8 years. They would be mortgage free 9.2 years sooner than anticipated.

The idea is to pay off the first mortgage completely. If they went with the increased payment of GBS 300, then in just under six years the property would be mortgage free.

Once the first mortgage is paid off, they will have the GBS 547 that they had been paying in mortgage payments on the first property in addition to any other funds that can now go towards paying off the second mortgage. Within 10 years, all the mortgages could be paid off completely.

Now the couple is 45 years old. Property values have risen a conservative 50% over the past 10 years. Here's the summary of their situation.

| | |
|---|---|
| Properties owned | 4 |
| Total value (50% on GBS 374,947) | 562,421 |
| Outstanding property loans | 0 |
| Equity | 562,421 |

Yes, I have had to make some assumptions, but at 45 years young, this couple has already made some sound choices. It's not a question of whether the capital appreciation ends higher or lower, it's about them having financial freedom. Unlike the majority of the working public, this couple will no longer be constrained by any future interest rate hikes. One thing that hasn't been accounted for yet is the rent. Over the past 10 years, rents would certainly have risen. This means that their actual cash flow would also have increased. At this stage, they could reinvest if desired, as they would still be eligible for a long-term mortgage—20 years, at least. They would also have an outstanding credit rating. How many people can claim that?

## 89 Some Golden Rules

I hope that you can begin to appreciate that when it comes to building a retirement nest egg for the future, property is still regarded as one of the safest long-term investments. However, there are some golden rules to consider before taking the plunge.

- **Have a plan.**

Have a clear plan to get started. Stick with the plan. At each milestone, create another plan if you must, but don't lose focus.

- **Know your budget.**

Use an income versus expenditure spreadsheet before investing in property. It's vital to have a thorough understanding of your cash flow. You can even ask your bank for pre-approval of your investment loan; that way you will know how much you're able to borrow before you start searching for properties.

- **Don't underestimate the costs.**

Budget enough for rates, insurance and general repairs. Remember, the older the property, the more likely repairs will be needed.

- **Seek growth areas.**

Seek an investment property in an area where there is strong demand for rental accommodation. Buying centrally located property near transport links, universities and schools will make it more attractive to renters. Remember the ripple effect.

- **Asset classes.**

Stick with one asset class to begin with. This could be residential, commercial, student housing, garages or renovation projects, for example.

- **Run the numbers.**

Buy with your head and not with your heart. Do the math, and don't get caught up in the emotion. Remember, you're buying as an investment, not as a place for you to live in. When visiting a potential property purchase, you need to look beyond any furniture and fittings and concentrate on the space and layout. Remember that a rental property should be clean and functional.

- **Negotiate.**

Almost every stage is negotiable. Even a fraction of a percentage here and there can soon add up to some palpable savings. Don't be afraid to put in low offers.

- **Use professionals.**

Don't shy away from seeking the help and services of brokers and property management companies. They can save you both time and money in the end.

- **Be confident.**

You must have confidence in yourself. It will be reflected in all levels of the process, especially when negotiating with people directly.

If you have read everything thus far, then you will appreciate that there is no magic formula. Property investing is certainly not a 'get-rich-quick scheme'. It's a long-term plan to secure financial freedom, and wealth is part of the equation. I am often asked what my plan is for the future. That's fine, I am happy to share; but make no mistake, what I do is based on where I live and my own personal goals. The property market is dynamic, so we all have to adapt. As you build your property portfolio, you will learn to do just that.

One of my goals is to build a *Grand Designs* house. I am an avid fan of the TV show and have watched every episode from its humble beginnings. In fact, hosting the program would probably be my dream job. You can sense the passion and feel the enthusiasm as each build comes to fruition. I take inspiration from each build, and over the years, I have managed to develop a dream home in my head—my own Grand Design, so to speak. The problem is, it keeps changing! So will I ever build it? Maybe. On the other hand, my passion and enthusiasm for investment property hasn't dwindled or changed in the slightest. So until the time comes, I will continue to invest in passive income properties.

Some 'property experts' will say that property investment is simple. The truth is that good property selection, financial discipline and a patient, long-term plan can mean a reasonably sized, debt free portfolio of properties in 15–25 years. For most investors starting in their late twenties or early thirties, this can mean financial freedom by their mid-forties. It's not a sophisticated plan—but it does work!

At the very start of this book, I posed a question: 'Please raise your hand if your answer is yes to the following question: if you could set a goal that would enable you to retire early while providing enough income to sustain your desired lifestyle, would you?' Did your hand go up? If so, let me ask a second question: Are you now motivated enough to start?

In conclusion, you must weigh both the risk and the reward before investing. As long as you are willing to educate yourself, understand the numbers and put it all into practice, then property investment is undoubtedly one of the best ways to create passive income and ultimately obtain financial freedom. Isn't that what we all want? You can put your hand down now and get started. 'Happy investing!'

# Glossary of Terms

**APR**

Annual percentage rate: The total cost of a loan, including all costs, interest charges and arrangement fees, shown as a percentage rate and easily comparable with mortgage interest rates.

**Auction**

The sale of a property to the highest bidder.

**Balance Outstanding**

The amount of a loan owed at a particular time.

**Bridging Loan**

A temporary loan advanced to help buy a new property before the first one has been sold.

**Buildings Insurance**

Insurance against the cost of repair or rebuilding a property from scratch following structural damage caused by fire, flood or storm, for example.

**Capitalisation Rate**

The ratio between the net operating income produced by an asset and its capital cost (the original price paid to buy the asset), or, its current market value.

**Cash-on-Cash**

The ratio of annual before-tax cash flow to the total amount of cash invested, expressed as a percentage

**Chain**

A number of linked property sales where the exchange of contracts must take place simultaneously.

**Closing Date**

The date set for the submission of offers when more than one party shows an interest in a property.

**Completion Date**

Completion of the legal transaction with all monies and documents having been distributed. This is also when the seller's solicitor will instruct the estate agent to release the keys.

**Contents Insurance**

Insurance against accidental damage or theft of all moveable contents, including furniture, appliances and soft furnishings.

**Contract**

A formal agreement between the buyer and the seller, usually prepared by a solicitor or licensed conveyancer, detailing the terms and conditions of the sale.

**Conveyancer**

Person other than a solicitor who may conduct the conveyancing.

**Conveyancing**

The legal work involved in buying and selling properties.

**Council Tax**

Levied by local councils to cover the costs of local amenities and services.

**Covenant**

A condition, contained within the title deeds or lease, with which the buyer must comply and which is usually applied to all future owners of the property. A restrictive covenant is one that prohibits the owner from doing something.

**Cross-collateralisation**

A term used when the collateral for one loan is also used as collateral for another loan.

**Deeds**

Legal documents assigning ownership of a property and/or land.

**Deposit**

Sum of money that represents the personal capital that the buyer is putting toward the purchase of the property.

**Disbursements**

Fees, such as stamp duty, land registry and search fees, which you normally pay on top of conveyancing via your solicitor or broker.

**Down Payment**

An initial payment made when something is bought on credit.

**Draft Contract**

Unconfirmed version of the contract.

**Early Repayment Charge**

A charge made by the lender if the borrower terminates a mortgage in advance of the terms of the particular mortgage. Normally occurs when the borrower has benefited from reduced payments or cash back in the early period of a mortgage.

**Equity**

The difference between the value of a property and the amount of mortgage owed.

**Fixed Price**

Offers are invited at the price shown.

**Fixtures and Fittings**

All non-structural items included in the purchase of a property.

**Freehold**

Ownership of the property and land upon which the property is situated.

**Full Structural Survey**

A full structural survey looks at all the main features of the property, including walls, roof, foundations, plumbing, joinery, electrical wiring, drains and garden.

**Gazumping**

The practice of a seller accepting a higher price from someone else than that which was previously agreed upon.

**Gazundering**

The practice of a buyer lowering his offer just before the exchange of contracts.

**Ground Rent**

The annual fee that a leaseholder pays to a freeholder.

**Home Buyer's Report**

The homebuyer's report comments on the structural condition of most parts of the property that are readily accessible but does not involve an in-depth investigation or the testing of water, drainage or heating systems.

**IFA**

Independent financial advisor.

**Instruction**

When a seller instructs an estate agent to market a property.

**Interest Rate**

The proportion of a loan that is charged as interest to the borrower, usually expressed as an annual percentage of the loan outstanding.

**Joint Agency**

Where two estate agents work together to market a property.

**Joint Mortgage**

A mortgage where there is more than one individual named responsible for the mortgage's repayment.

**Land Certificate**

A land registry certificate proving ownership of property.

**Land Registry**

Typically a government organisation that holds records of all registered properties.

**Leasehold**

To be given ownership of a property but not the land it is built on. This normally requires the payment of ground rent to the landlord. A leasehold is normally offered for either 999 years, 99 years or shorter terms.

**Lien**

A lien is a form of security interest granted over an item of property to secure the payment of a debt or the performance of some other.

**Loan Term**

The period you need to repay the loan.

**Local Authority Search**

An application made to the appropriate local authority requesting details of any planning or other matters that might affect the property being sold.

**Maintenance Charge**

A charge made towards the upkeep of a leasehold property.

**Mortgage Deed**

A legal document relating to the mortgage lender's interest in the property.

**Mortgage Offer**

A formal written offer made by a bank or building society to lend an approved amount to purchase a property.

**Multi-agency**

The selection of two or more estate agents to act on the seller's behalf, usually incurring a higher fee than if the sale were completed by a single agency.

**Negative Equity**

When the value of a property is less than the outstanding sum owed on a mortgage.

**Net Income**

Net operating income (NOI) is a calculation used to analyse property investments that generate income. NOI equals all revenue from the property minus all reasonably necessary operating expenses.

**Non-Amortised**

A type of loan in which payments on the principal are not made, while interest payments or minimum payments are made regularly. The principal is then paid as a lump sum at the maturity of the loan.

**Offer**

A bid made by a prospective buyer; this is not legally binding in many countries.

**Offers Over**

Offers are invited above the price shown.

**Off-plan**

The selling or purchasing of property before the property is built and with only the plans available for inspection.

**Ombudsman**

Independent professional bodies that investigate complaints on behalf of customers against estate agents, solicitors and insurance companies.

**Other Income**

All the other income generated from the property.

**Part-possession**

The term used when a property is being sold, where a tenant has legal right of occupation.

**Purchase Price**

The price of the real property.

**Real Estate**

Property consisting of land or buildings.

**Repayment Mortgage**

Your monthly repayment includes part interest and part capital repayment. So long as you meet on time all the payments required by the lender, your mortgage will gradually reduce until it is repaid in full at the end of the mortgage term.

**Repossession**

When loans are in default, the mortgage lender can repossess the property and sell it so they can recover the debt.

**Retention**

Holding back part of a mortgage loan until repairs to the property are satisfactorily completed.

**Sale Agreed**

An oral agreement from the seller.

**Searches**

Checks of local council records for planning applications and restrictions etc.

**Sole Agency**

The seller chooses a single estate agent to act on their behalf, thus incurring a lower fee than multi-agency.

**Solicitor**

Legal expert handling all documentation for the sale and purchase of a property.

**Stamp Duty**

Applicable in certain countries, this tax is paid to the government by the buyer upon completion.

**Tenants**

People living in a property owned by someone else.

**Tender**

The process whereby the seller asks for written offers on a property, usually with a set closing date. When a property is sold by tender, the buyer pays the fees.

**Title or Title Deed**

The ultimate record of ownership of a property, the evidence of which is found in the title deeds.

**Transfer Deeds**

The land registry document that transfers legal ownership from seller to buyer.

**Under Offer**

When the seller has accepted an offer on the property but contracts have not yet been exchanged.

**Variable Interest Rate**

Rate of interest payment that fluctuates over time in line with general interest rates.

**Vendor**

The legal term sometimes used to describe the seller of the property.

**Verbal Offer**

Offer from a prospective purchaser, not legally binding on either party.

**Writ**

Mode of commencing legal proceedings.

www.ingramcontent.com/pod-product-compliance
Lightning Source LLC
Chambersburg PA
CBHW071416180526
45170CB00001B/118